1. PINK AND GREEN *Edgar Degas*

Degas has used rich, glowing color in this informal
version of one of his favorite themes.

Exploring
Art

BY LUISE C. KAINZ M.A.

CHAIRMAN OF ART DEPARTMENT

BAY RIDGE HIGH SCHOOL, NEW YORK CITY

AND OLIVE L. RILEY M.A.

DIRECTOR OF ART

BOARD OF EDUCATION, NEW YORK CITY

NEW YORK · CHICAGO

HARCOURT, BRACE AND COMPANY

PREFACE

THE ULTIMATE aim of secondary school education is to develop a complete and rounded personality. How does the Art Education Program contribute to this goal? We believe that its most important contribution lies in making the student realize that he must (1) observe keenly and react vividly; (2) develop memory and imagination; (3) exercise judgment and discrimination; (4) express ideas courageously and logically; and (5) construct with power and with vision.

The student who has acquired these abilities through active classroom practice will be well equipped to confront the opportunities that present themselves after high school and will regard them as a challenge, for he has a foundation for independent judgment that will serve him well.

Curiosity, imagination, and inventiveness can be aroused, provided that the student has a lively and sincere interest in adding these qualities to his native equipment. A true appreciation of form, of color, and of design can be developed if he is allowed to play an active, not a passive, part in his own educative processes. A love of beauty cannot be engendered in him solely by exposing him to culture but must come through personal experience and personal understanding of the qualities that he himself has struggled to attain. It is our task to develop good taste and spirited, honest production of things suited to daily living. If we arouse interest in all branches of " doing," we shall finally develop a group of citizens who are able to make an independent evaluation of the contributions of the present and of the past.

Culture cannot develop on the artificial nourishment of verbose authorities or through a preoccupation with past accomplishment. Culture develops through the life and strength of each individual and each community throughout the nation. In the past all forms of art were a part of daily living. We must do everything to make these expressions of art live today. Tying them down with dates, facts, and anecdotes robs them of meaning for the student at this stage in his development. We must give equal value to all forms of living art and make contemporary or past examples function as one natural expression.

The Art Appreciation Program

Art Appreciation touches the life of the student at a time when he is most receptive and most sensitive. A fine, far-reaching, progressive Art Appreciation Program has possibilities for becoming a powerful and educative force in his life.

Unceasing efforts are being made by educators to equip students to meet their responsibilities in the world. To aid this purpose art teachers have maintained a program that is fluid and sensitive to all things. It is their faith in the future that makes them plan, reject, then plan again. Building on the past, they have used the best that has gone before as a foundation for loftier, more ambitious, idealized, yet practical structures. By constant striving they hope to create, through the individual, a finer, better, more enjoyable world.

In the relatively brief time since its inception, the Art Appreciation Program has traveled a long road with remarkable speed. Once the days of drawing for all students were over, the concept of Art Appreciation developed rapidly into a force with many possibilities and implications.

Gradually we have arrived at a turn in the road where we should pause and review the recent events in our travels — the difficulties overcome and the things achieved. Have we changed our methods of travel? Have we shifted or discarded excess baggage or added new weight to our load? Is our ultimate destination a new goal?

The answer to these questions is, of course, yes. Teachers and students have deserted some of the familiar paths and are finding new ones. They have become explorers rather than mere followers of the path and are seeking new goals, new and more ambitious destinations. This broadening of our aims makes many demands upon our mental and our physical equipment.

How do these aims differ from the old? Are they sharply at variance with them? Specifically the change is threefold, involving aims, methods of procedure, and organization of subject matter.

The *aims* of the Art Appreciation Course are (1) to aid the student in the development of a complete and rounded personality; (2) to equip him for active, full participation in the life of the community; and (3) to foster in him a love of art and to make him sensitive to it in all its forms.

Through Art Appreciation the individual is aided in attaining full mental, spiritual, and esthetic growth.

Through Art Appreciation the individual becomes an integral part of the community. The ideal member of a community is both constructive and selective. He either creates, or he recognizes esthetically fine expression and rejects that which is only fashionable or sensational.

Through Art Appreciation the individual learns to appreciate art in all its forms and to recognize art as a force which has always shaped the lives and destinies of mankind.

The *fundamental procedures* of the Art Appreciation Course are (1) teaching the student to recognize and to understand the underlying structure common to all forms of art; (2) helping the student to learn through personal experience; and (3) teaching the student to realize the importance of each experience as a link in the chain of his knowledge.

In Art Appreciation the student first meets the general problem — understanding art as a whole — in the simplest way. Formerly he met isolated examples of art carefully selected by the teacher.

This awareness of the whole, of art as an entity, is accomplished by centering each term's work * around an integrating force. In the first term this force is *color;* in the second it is *form.*

The Study of Color and of Form

A study of color fosters an understanding of all the things with which color is concerned: line and line movement, mass, tone, quality, quantity,

* The Art Appreciation Course, which is required for graduation in many States, is generally scheduled in the ninth year. For those schools in which it is taught for four terms, it is assumed that A.A.I and II are equivalent to A.A.I, and that A.A.III and IV are equivalent to A.A.II.

placing, emotional effects of hues, of values, of intensities, etc. These qualities are studied not as separate and detached units but are seen in their relation to color in particular and to the specific art problem as a whole.

Similarly, a study of form, or three-dimensional art, is based upon the unity of all qualities with which form is concerned: line movement, proportion, balance, space, volume, as well as with color. These qualities are emphasized as important only in their relation to the entire structure of form. An understanding of this unity leads to an appreciation of the practical phases of living.

Throughout the course the student works to gain from the problem or the particular exercise knowledge which he can add to his previously acquired experiences, rather than to achieve a finished product.

The student learns through his own experiences rather than through those of others. His exercises are personal excursions through which he makes his own discoveries and draws his own conclusions in contrast to those which are given merely to illustrate a rule, a principle, a definition.

The Exploratory Period

Each term's work is begun with an exploratory period of four weeks. At this time the student is given a series of brief, daily exercises which are designed by the teacher to reveal to him the essentials: the structure, the necessary unity and the organization of color and of form.

These exercises are not to be thought of as finished products but are used as a testing ground for the student's development. Teacher and pupil explore, discover, then clarify their discoveries. This searching, this attempt to grasp the fundamental rather than the superficial aspects of art, continues consistently throughout the course, even when the student is working in definite fields.

During this exploratory period discussion takes place both during the lesson and at its conclusion. In addition, there should be an evaluation period after a certain number of exercises, perhaps three, which should include the following: (1) Evaluation by the student of his own growth in understanding and in power of expression. (2) Review of discoveries and their meaning. (3) Appreciation of works of art in the light of the student's discoveries. (4) Acquisition of appropriate terminology and development of broad concepts of art terms. (5) Practice in the vocabulary of art by the students through discussion in the activities mentioned above.

Application of Knowledge

Application of knowledge to fields of interest follows. The student constantly explores the field, not with the aim of achieving a work of art, but of discovering the fundamental structure of each field.

At this time the teacher must be especially careful not to encumber the problem with a mass of practical facts and considerations. It must be stripped of any complications that would tend to obstruct the student's perception of the problem as primarily one of color, of form, or of both.

The *organization of the subject matter* of Art Appreciation consists of the following: (1) It embraces all the main fields of art. (2) The first term's work is concerned with the study of color in painting, in the theater, in advertising, in costume design, and in interior design, and with the specific character of the graphic arts. (3) The second term's work is concerned with the study of form in relation to sculpture, to industrial design, to architecture, and to the community, and with the particular nature of the crafts.

The subject matter of Art Appreciation is based upon present and past expressions of art that are within the student's range of interest and of living. It is organized so as to bring all expressions of art under two broad elements — color and form. This method of organization allows for great freedom in assembling material for study from any time or period, race or culture, material or technique. The final fusion of these two elements results in the concept of art as a whole.

During the exploratory period much of the subject matter is abstract. Abstract subject matter avoids the demands and the entanglements of a special application, such as costume, interiors, or posters. This plan is a departure from the days when subject matter was used as motivation, to make the work attractive to the student, to make him feel accomplished, an " artist," even though the things he produced had only superficial meaning.

After the experiences of the exploratory period the student should be prepared to meet the problems of a particular field because of his enriched background. The sequence of such problems varies with the student's interests and his needs. The teacher must so shape the course that every essential area is covered. Work in Art Appreciation has been greatly weakened in the past because teachers emphasized poster work, commercial design, craft work, and similar limited phases of art at the expense of broader and more important fields.

Illustrative Materials and How to Use Them

Illustrative material plays an important part in the Art Appreciation Course. It ranges from the traditional to the contemporary, and includes a limitless variety of expressions.

Formerly, a collection of illustrative material was shown in order to impress the student with accepted works of art. In this course all fields of the present as well as of the past are considered. Even simple and familiar things, such as children's building blocks, are as helpful in starting a discussion as a picture of Radio City; colored Easter eggs are as interesting as a majolica vase. A student's own work may well serve him as a key to unlock the world of painting throughout the ages.

A collection of illustrative material, built up by contributions from students as well as from experienced teachers, will help to make every discovery, every discussion, every creation a vital one. This collection of illustrative material might be used in demonstration work, or in group problems, as an occasional substitute for the work of individual students.

The illustrations in this book have been chosen and assembled with the idea that there is no gap in time or in manner of expression which sets one creation apart from another. Each is an added proof of man's tremendous range of expression.

Since a ninth-year student in most cases has not had a background of history and therefore has no way of realizing an historic example in relation to its particular civilization, let him become aware first of the value of each expression of art as such. Let it serve as the direct inspiration for his own activities, rather than as an example of other people's activities in the past. The historic aspect may be stressed in history classes later, and in Advanced Art Appreciation classes in the senior year.

The Role of the Teacher of Art

To realize the aims of the Art Appreciation Course we must have art teachers of courage and of vision, teachers who are resourceful and imaginative; in brief, teachers who have the qualities which they desire to find in their students. We must have teachers who are ready and willing to step off the platform down to the classroom floor to take part in the group experience.

To accomplish the aims of the Art Appreciation Course they must be willing, even anxious, to strip art of all its frills, of all its " busy work," of all but its essential structure; to strip it of its fatty accumulation, its verbosity concerning dates and historic facts, " arty " irrelevancies and mysterious hocus pocus; to take it out of fancy aprons and put it into overalls to do the spade work necessary for building a better, finer, and more livable world.

This book received impetus from the work of the Art Appreciation Committee, appointed by Miss Virginia Murphy, Director of Art in the New York City schools, and from the experimental work of the teachers of art of New York City. We wish to express our appreciation of the valuable work of these teachers, together with that of the members of the Committee with whom we worked: Miss Muriel Adams, Miss Jole Angeletti, Mrs. Madeleine Bowles, Miss Florence Gough, Mrs. Helen Gray, Mrs. Yvonne Grodin, Mr. Joseph Grosse, Miss Florence Harrison, Miss Helen Hird, Miss Ruth McEvoy, Mrs. Catherine Osheridan, Miss Mary Ellen Ragan, Mr. Fred Wichman, Mrs. Helen Wiltsey, as well as that of the secretarial assistant, Mrs. Etta Bardwell.

We wish to thank Dr. Helen H. Tanzer for many fruitful suggestions and for her kindness in reading our book in manuscript and again in proof.

L. C. K.
O. L. R.

CONTENTS

ILLUSTRATIONS

xvi

xviii

xxii

xxiii

xxiv

1.

HOW TO STUDY

ART

IF THERE WERE an old chest stored away in the attic and if after many years you were to come upon it, how exciting that would be. Old books to read, photographs to look at, or a calendar to study; elaborate dresses, fancy hats, an old sword, tools or gadgets might start you off on some invention of your own. Unused or unfamiliar materials make us think; they challenge us to make use of them.

We all have within ourselves a treasure chest which contains our undeveloped qualities. They are our hidden abilities, our aptitudes and interests. It is for us to discover these qualities, to exercise and to strengthen them.

Exercise Your Abilities

The athlete strengthens his muscles and nervous reflexes by patient exercise so that they will work together at his will. If you were to tie back your arm and leave it tied for a long time it would become useless. In just such a way your mental abilities will become stunted or will even disappear if they are not allowed to work fully and freely. Human beings are equipped with fine machines for thinking and for doing, but often they allow certain parts of these machines to become rusty or to fall into disuse.

Now Is Your Opportunity

The opportunity of trying yourself out, of realizing your powers, is offered to you during your high-school life. The study of art is especially a

I

field for thorough exercise. Rich, exciting, and satisfying, it can play a great part in developing you as a personality, as an artist, and as a leader in your world.

What can you do to develop your capabilities? What exercises will assist in your development?

Be Observant

Begin by observing the world around you. Look carefully at people, at places, and at objects. Notice colors, shapes, proportions, forms, and their relation to one another. Look for movement, for pattern. Look for the plan of the whole and the quality of the whole. To train the eye to see into, around, and through things, to develop an awareness that misses nothing is to learn the path to quick thinking and sure decisions.

Develop Your Memory and Your Imagination

All that you observe and picture in your mind becomes a part of your storehouse of knowledge. Try to see clearly and to remember what you see. In detective stories we read of the man with the hawklike glance, with the camera eye that records not only keenly but permanently. In place of the blurry, hazy focus, the hasty glance, you, too, should try to substitute the sharp and complete picture which you can recall at will. Train yourself to remember what things look like, how they are constructed, how they move.

Learn to let your imagination play with all the things you have seen and can remember. Combine these things to make new color combinations and new forms; put them to new uses. Try to be original and inventive in your thinking. Discard ideas that are easily formed and commonplace. Remember that imagination is one of the greatest assets of the artist.

Good Judgment Is Important

Every time you select or create a line, a shape, a color, or a form, take the time to consider it in relation to the other lines, shapes, colors, or forms with which it is concerned. Consider how to improve it. Even the simplest choices require judgment and thought. Both fine things and worthless things are shown to us as art. We must learn to recognize and to select what is best.

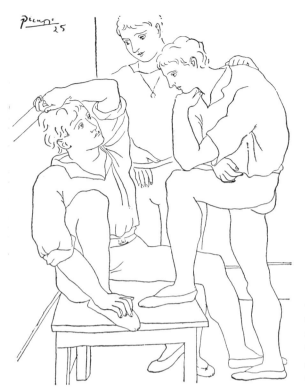

This contour, or outline, drawing is by Picasso, the modern Spanish-born artist. The simple, forceful line and striking pose record an impression of vitality and action, even though the figures are in repose.

2. THREE DANCERS RESTING *Pablo Picasso*

Skilled craftsmen of long ago made pottery for everyday use and, in ways suitable and original, they decorated their products with scenes from the life about them. On this fragment, we see a version of a remembered hunting scene, which is boldly executed.

3

3. DETAIL FROM AN AEGEAN VASE *1350* B.C.–*1100* B.C.

4. DRAWING *Unknown Japanese artist*

Through constant observation and drawing of familiar things, this artist was enabled to make a beautiful brush drawing of so humble a subject as a mouse. He stored in his memory the lively curiosity and darting movements of this tiny creature and used excellent judgment in selecting and setting down the lines that would best express them.

Through a study of art a boy learned to see his neighborhood with new interest. His block print makes good use of the unusual patterns and textures which he saw in an old house turned over to the pigeons. Do you not think that he used his abilities to produce something truly original?

5. BIRD HOUSE *Student work*

Express Yourself Clearly

Train yourself to express your ideas clearly, logically, and courageously, not only on paper and with tools, but also in words. Welcome every opportunity to take part in activities in school or out that will help you to have confidence in yourself. Art students have the reputation of being shy, of " taking a back seat," because they are likely to be timid about expressing their ideas in words. You must use words as well as hands to make art effective in the world.

Construct with Will Power and Vision

Above all, use your abilities. Your observation of the interesting or unusual things about you should encourage you to work on problems of your own. Be an active artist; a creator, not a dreamer. Instead of spending hours in the movies or on the street, spend some of that time doing things, making things for yourself and for others. It is more fun to step out of the audience and to take part in the play than it is to be a spectator. It is better to make a world of your own than to accept one that is ready-made.

Be Original

To be an independent thinker in any field means that you must avoid parrotlike repetition. That, in art, means copying. When copying, the average student takes the nearest, easiest thing at hand, such as newspaper strips or magazine illustrations. Such printed matter is seldom art, nothing is gained by copying it. The ease with which some students can copy or repeat pictures is not a true sign of ability. True ability in art is the power to invent, to create, to design with originality.

Art Leads to Creative Thinking

Many of us think of art only as painting, architecture, and sculpture. We do not realize that the branches of art have grown steadily and have developed in directions that lead to new undertakings, new responsibilities, and new materials invented by man and put to his own use. Modern life is a challenge to the artist. For this reason the field of art, reaching into man's every enterprise, has been enriched and expanded by his spirited and im-

The famous French painter of the nineteenth century, Degas, was interested in making intensive studies of ballet dancers at work. His pastel drawing reveals the power and vitality of his work and shows how far he goes beyond depicting merely the pretty aspect of the dancers. In preparation for a painting of this subject, such as we see in illustration 1, Degas made countless studies of his models.

6. BALLET DANCER   *Edgar Degas*

The dance is always an appealing and popular form of expression. Here the Hopi Indian, with his love of this art, has painted a highly imaginative, rhythmic design. The quaint figure has a graceful and childlike quality.

7. DANCING SQUASH   *Hopi Indian*

8. BRIDGE AT TRINQUETAILLE *Vincent van Gogh*

Van Gogh, the modern Dutch artist, painted an intensely vivid picture of a
scene in France where he often worked. Compare it with the photograph
below of the same scene and you will see how he interpreted it in his own
way. Both his design and his color emphasize the character of the scene
and bring it to life in a manner quite different from that of the camera.

9. BRIDGE AT TRINQUETAILLE *John Rewald*

aginative thinking. To make your contribution to art you must be ready to approach all its phases with an active and inquiring mind.

Misconceptions about Art

How often have you said or heard from others, " I'm no artist. I can't even draw a straight line," or, " Don't expect me to try that. You know I can't draw! " In your work in Art Appreciation the ability to draw accurately is not important, for drawing is only one of the many ways in which ideas can be expressed. The idea, rather than the means by which you choose to express it, is the important thing.

From fairy tales and movies we have come to think of the artist as a picturesque sort of fellow in smock and beret, searching the world over for a perfect model, or starving quietly in his garret. This is a romantic description, but it is pure fancy. Some artists have led unusual lives, but most of them have been as sane and sound, as down to earth as you or I, possibly even more so. Let us think of the artist as a normal human being with unusual vision and power.

Nearly all art work can be understood in one way or another. Unfortunately, the things we do not understand we are inclined to ridicule. Haven't we all heard at some exhibition at some time or other, " Why, any four-year-old child could do better than that? " Let us reserve our judgment about the paintings, sculpture, and buildings that we do not understand, or the things that an artist has created solely for his personal satisfaction until we have a background of knowledge and understanding with which to accept or to reject them.

Art Brings Enjoyment and Satisfaction

To know and to understand art in its many forms brings lasting pleasure, a pleasure that grows richer and fuller as we grow in understanding. Some of us are active artists who create. Others are passive artists who understand and appreciate the work of others. All of us can enjoy art in one form or other and all of us should be vitally interested in art throughout our lives. Art enables us to realize our possibilities as individuals, working together, playing together, striving together both spiritually and practically to build a finer and more enjoyable world.

10. THE ADMIRAL'S WIFE *Rembrandt van Rijn*

This Dutch artist of the seventeenth century used his remarkable powers of observation to portray people. His oil painting shows how he used dramatic color, luminous light, and dark not only to portray the appearance but also to capture the personality of his subject.

2.

MEANING
AND STRUCTURE
OF ART

CHILDREN NEARLY ALWAYS enjoy scribbling, coloring, and painting fantastic pictures; they find fun in whittling, carving, and building forts, castles, ships, or airplanes. They do these things as instinctively as a baby reaches for a brightly colored object. A child may be limited in words, but he delights in making crayon scrawls. Later these scrawls take on a meaning that his parents can understand. It is the beginning of a natural form of communication.

Through a study of art we can see again the early ages of civilization. At a time when man's speech was not developed enough to express all his thoughts, he relied on art forms to record his history. Living under dangerous conditions, he was exposed to the severities of climate and the hardships of nature. There was much that he had to tell that excited or troubled him. The success of his hunt for food and the results of his battles were great moments in his life, but hunting and fighting were not enough to satisfy him. Early man desired to make a record of what he did, to express visually his hopes, his fears, and his reactions to his environment.

Such are the promptings that make art expressions and art forms eternal! Thus have individuals, groups, and races of men in totally different parts of the world arrived at some characteristic form of recording or of constructing into visible form their beliefs, their feelings, their activities, and their very enjoyment of life.

9

Art Is Everlasting

Those of you who know the fun of a treasure hunt can understand the thrill experienced by professional treasure hunters like the archeologists who dig deep in the earth searching for records of past civilizations. In all parts of the world they have found lost cities, temples, and tombs, and even the humble dwellings of early man. By studying simple objects made of stone, clay, or wood, as well as the more ambitious structures left by early man, we may learn about his existence, his physical life, his appearance, his dress, his food and drink, and also about his work, his play, and his religious life.

Those who interpret early man through the things he created, through the art that he has left for us to see and to enjoy, receive deep spiritual hope and joy from the continuous urge of mankind to create. They know that forms of art may be created, or destroyed, or reconstructed and destroyed again, but that the qualities in these forms are as everlasting as the spirit within the human body.

Art Is a Universal Language

Art is a language common to all men. It invites exploration since it transports us to all parts of the world and to all periods of time. It explains the people of the past to us as well as those of the present, and it will speak for us to future generations. This language is universally understandable because of its structure, in spite of human variations in ideas, in habits, and in customs. In its simplest form art is a language we all use; in its complex form it has become the most expressive language of all.

The Structure of the Language of Art

What is the structure of the language of art? Shall we try to find the elements with which it is built? For this search the one essential tool you must have is the power of observation. Without it you will lose your way easily and find yourself depending on the opinions of others rather than on your own.

This symbolic painting from the Libyan Desert reveals a primitive artist's conception of the relative size and importance of a god and of mankind. How small and insignificant the figures appear in comparison with the hand! The painting carries a thought that will be clear to people of all times and shows that art is a direct means of expressing man's eternal belief in a spiritual power.

11. HAND AND THREE FIGURES *Prehistoric*

This small mural painting from a cave in Spain was made with the crude tools and materials that were available in early days. It shows a remarkable feeling for an exciting subject and a great capacity for expressing swift movement. Notice that the artist used flat, or silhouetted figures, with great effect.

12. STAG HUNT *Prehistoric*

These two records of primitive man's love of art are an Indian stone pipe, found in Ohio, and a wall painting. While the former was designed for practical use, it also satisfied the carver's desire to produce a beautiful figure. The bison, which was painted on the wall of a deep cave in Spain centuries ago, in prehistoric times, shows remarkable power of observation and of memory. In making the painting the artist worked by the light of a tiny stone lamp and used brushes and paints that he himself had made. Contrast this mural with illustration 12. How do they differ?

13. STONE PIPE *Prehistoric*

14. BISON COW *Prehistoric*

15. STREET SCENE *Maurice de Vlaminck*

Artists have always been interested in their surroundings, finding in them things that most people would overlook. This simple street scene impressed Vlaminck, the French painter, with the beauty of its color.

16. CARD PLAYERS *Paul Cézanne*

In this painting, Cézanne, one of the greatest of the modern French painters, relied largely on color to interpret for him his reactions to the scene. Notice how solid the figures are and how compactly they are grouped.

Start Your Search with Familiar Objects

What are the elements that appear again and again in every work of art? Observe with interest, for example, a collection of familiar objects. Which one attracts you the most? Pick it up and study it carefully. Are you pleased by its color, its shape, its size, its form, or by a combination of all of these things? In almost every case the color attracts you first.

Color Is a Basic Element

Color has instantaneous power. For this reason it is an important element in the structure of art. In the studies we shall make, color will be one of the main roads to follow. The more color you observe along the way, the more you will appreciate its variety and richness. The number of colors, the range from light to dark and from bright to dull, their combinations, their fluid and sensitive qualities are all of great importance to you in building a rich structure of color.

Form Is the Other Basic Element

If you look carefully at an object, you will become aware of its form. This form may be simple and basic like a sphere, a cylinder, or a cube, or it may be complex because several basic forms have been combined. Objects may be as huge as the Empire State building or as tiny as a bead. They vary endlessly in size, in shape, and in proportions. An object, such as a vase or a gas tank may be hollow or it may be solid like a baseball bat or a pyramid. It may have divisions within it, like a chest of drawers or a house. Whether simple or complex, useful or purely ornamental, the beauty of all objects is determined by the beauty of their *proportions;* that is, by the relation of their various parts to the whole and to one another.

Color and Form Are Concerned with Texture

Surface quality, or texture, is common to both color and form. Texture is due to the nature of the material itself, as that of ivory, stone, wool, and paper, or it may be the result of varying treatment. For example, paper may be corrugated or sanded, stone may be roughened or made smooth. The texture of dress material, to a large extent is the result of the

13

Cylindrical forms have many variations and serve many purposes. For example, these tremendous turbines, designed to be driven by water and to generate power, are impressive for their simplicity, their size, and suggestion of strength.

These water tanks, though built solely to serve a practical need, are interesting for their size and for their proportion. Their simple, cylindrical form is a fundamental one. The shed in the foreground, a contrasting form, is a rectangular block, although not completely enclosed.

17. TURBINES

18. WATER TANK

This section of a modern house, with its large expanse of wall space, is both beautiful and functional in its simple, rectangular block form. Notice how esthetically satisfying it is.

These tanks are remarkable for their size and the simplicity of their form. The artist photographed them at the moment when the light intensified not only their spherical form but also their texture. The contrasting pattern made by the light and the dark shadows is dramatic.

19. BRAZILIAN HOUSE

20. AVIATION GAS   *I. K. Morehouse*

21. ROAD RUNNER *Eliot Porter*

The rough cactus in one photograph and the smooth seaweed in the other present marked contrast in texture. The curious and exciting combinations of textures in nature are often intensified by photographs which reveal far more than the human eye could ever see unaided.

22. KELP *Edward Weston*

The infinite variety of texture to be found in nature suggested to a young student this experiment with leaves, feathers, and grasses. The contrasting surfaces she arranged make an interesting and richly textured design.

The rugged earth presents a surface of unusual pattern. The camera caught and accentuated fascinating textures that are ordinarily difficult to see.

23. TEXTURES *Student work*

24. ELK BASIN, WYOMING

particular weaving process used. The texture of an object adds to our enjoyment, often making us wish to touch it or to take it into our hands, in order to enjoy more fully its particular quality. Texture affects color quality. Two pieces of material, one rough and the other smooth, may be dyed with the same color, yet they will not be identical in color for they reflect or absorb light differently. Texture also affects the apparent size of objects. For example, a small glass object, because of its light-catching surface, may appear larger than an object of the same size with a dull finish. Varieties in texture have been used by artists throughout all ages to heighten our enjoyment of color and of form.

How Shall We Use the Basic Elements?

We have noted that the basic elements of the structure of art are color and form. It is now time to find out how these elements can create a work of art. They can do so only when their combination results in perfect harmony and unity. To aid us in attaining this perfect relationship, we have four guides: the qualities of *rhythm,* of *balance,* of *emphasis,* and of *proportion.*

Of these four qualities, rhythm is the one with which you are most familiar. Do not the waves of the ocean have great fascination for you? The onrushing crest of each wave makes us want to linger, to see, and to enjoy the next one and the next. The feeling of movement you experience when in a swing or on a merry-go-round is a pleasant sensation. Those of you who enjoy dancing do so because you know how to move in harmony with the music. When we speak of rhythm in art we are referring to a varied repetition of colors and forms. Repetition creates a sensation of movement. Thus, it is possible to have color arrangements that seem to carry the eye along a delightful path of varying colors. The thoughtful repetition, or movement, of color in a room illustrates a practical application of the power of rhythm in color arrangements, for by a use of this quality our eyes travel with pleasure to all parts of a well-designed room.

Objects, as well as colors, may have the quality of rhythm, or, as it is sometimes called, rhythmical movement. A bridge may excite our admiration of the rhythm of its span. Modern automobiles and streamlined trains have a beauty which comes from the harmonious flow of all parts into one another. To sum up, we may say that rhythm is the quality that gives movement and life to color and to form.

25. RADIO TRANSMISSION TOWER

This is an example of an open form, a prism, which serves an important need. Slender and very high, it seems as impressive as a church spire. The repetition of its structural elements emphasizes the upward movement.

26. PAINTED CHEST *Unknown Pennsylvania Dutch artist*

Notice that the decorations on this wooden chest are similar, and that within each one we find a formal balance of the motif. The Pennsylvania Dutch artist who decorated it obviously liked designs to be evenly balanced. Refer to illustration 146 to see the work of a sculptor who also used this type of balance for his figure. In contrast, the painted panel below shows how a New Mexico craftsman took pleasure in freely balanced lines and tones. In illustration 143, you will see the work of a sculptor who also used informal balance in his design.

27. PANEL FROM CHEST *Unknown New Mexican artist*

Putting things in order is instinctive with most of us. Setting a table, arranging articles in a desk, or planting different kinds of seeds in rows satisfies our feeling for organization and for beauty. When we make such an arrangement, we are inclined in some way to match, or balance things. Our sense of order calls for balanced colors and balanced forms. When we see a woman instinctively straighten a picture on a wall, or a man adjust a necktie that is awry, we realize that they are doing so because their feeling for balance has been disturbed.

Balance is a quality that may be very apparent or may be hidden and subtle. An even, or formal, balance of color and of form is satisfying and easy to feel. The human figure is a good example of this kind of balance. Uneven, or informal, balance is less obvious because it is accomplished through subtle variations in colors and in forms. Countless paintings and pieces of sculpture, for example, owe their beauty to a sensitive use of the quality of balance.

Variety in things around us and unusual touches of one kind or another attract our attention. One hardly notices, for example, the bare walls of a long, school corridor until someone hangs two or three large, brilliant paintings or posters on them. Immediately the entire corridor is transformed, for now it has sections that attract our attention in a forceful way. There are any number of means by which a designer or an artist can bring out a particular shape in a design or a part of an object which he may wish to emphasize. By stressing the color, the texture, or the size of some section, he makes it especially interesting and attractive. To sum up, emphasis may be considered that quality which brings out some special part of a design.

In studying a work of art to determine its inherent qualities, we naturally consider its proportions. In color we compare the amounts and kinds of color to determine whether their relationships are pleasing. In objects we judge the relationships of height and length, breadth and depth, weight and size. When you have trained yourself to study and to compare the proportions of all things that interest you, then you will be able to select with judgment and good taste. In whatever you plan to paint, to design, to model or to construct, there will be constant need for you to consider the quality of proportion.

Understanding Develops through Constant Observation

We have said that you must observe keenly in order to recognize the qualities that make for beauty. The more you observe, the better you will be able to enjoy and to evaluate what you see. A drinking glass or a piece of sculpture, the house you live in, the walls you look at, the paintings on the walls, all are composed of the same basic art elements. The more you use the language of art in your daily life, the more you will be able to enjoy the beauty in the world about you.

28. EXPERIMENTS IN COLOR

These daubs of paint, placed directly on paper, are exciting and full of interest. Colors move, express a range of moods from gay to somber, and create various harmonies.

3.

EXPERIMENTS
IN COLOR

THE LANGUAGE of art gives us, as individuals, opportunity for expression. To use this language freely we must pick up the thread of our childhood when our fears were few and our courage high. How shall we begin our experiments?

Start with Color

Color and movement are two things we recognize early in life. To use color directly is to learn the language of art in its liveliest, most vivid, and most natural form. To start with color is to begin in the field which is the richest and most adventuresome for exploration.

How shall we use color? First, we shall allow color to speak for itself. Let us try to find out what color is, what it does, and how it affects us; what we can do with it; how we can use it to create qualities and moods. Then we shall be ready to create color harmonies for a definite use, such as for a poster or a stage design; or to create them for individual expression, such as for costume or interiors. Throughout our work we mean to think independently about color, to arrive at personal conclusions only after experimentation with it.

As you work you will soon discover that to use color well depends on your understanding of all its qualities. Quality and refinement in your use of color are developed by experimenting with it. Every trial will be a valuable experience that will gradually lead to an understanding of the importance of color, what it is, what it does, and the part it plays in our lives.

Are you eager to work in color, without further delay? If so, we have some suggestions for you.

Look for Color

Begin by collecting bits of paper, fancy wrapping papers, pages from old magazines, odds and ends of cloth, and similar scraps that have a good deal of color in them. You may also include black and white among your colors. Examine your collection to make sure that you have a variety of colors — some light and others dark, some bright and others dull. Exchange scraps with your classmates so that each collection may be richer and more varied.

Experiment with Your Collection

Spread your collection out on a black, white, tan, or gray background. Select a few colors that are pleasing or attractive to you. Cut or fold the scraps or pieces of material so that you have an assortment of large and small pieces of color in various shapes.

Place these pieces on the background. Let some of them touch or overlap. Move them about, discarding here and there, and adding pieces until you are pleased with the whole arrangement of colors.

Ask Yourself Questions about Your Experiment

1. Does the combination of colors create a feeling of movement?
2. If so, what kind of movement? Does it flow up, down, or around? Does it move gracefully, swiftly, or slowly? Does it rush, dart, or leap about?
3. Does the feeling of movement come from the colors themselves? From the way you have placed them in relation to one another? Or from a combination of color and arrangement?
4. If there is a lack of movement in your arrangement, is it because it has too much of an even, all-over effect? Does it seem to be monotonous?
5. Is this monotonous effect produced because the colors are too much alike in size and in shape?

Sum Up Your Discoveries

Color moves. The selection and grouping of colors can be planned so that the eye moves easily along certain paths or directions throughout the entire arrangement. This quality of movement which brings life to color and makes it pleasing to the eye is called color *rhythm*.

Improve and Complete Your Experiment

Make any changes you now think desirable in your color arrangement. Observe it from a distance and from various angles before you make your final decisions. Paste the colored pieces carefully on the background. Now, as well as in the future, take pride in the way you complete your work. All ideas are worth being carefully presented.

Review the Results Obtained by the Class

Can you find examples of any particular kind of color movement, or color rhythm, such as calm, violent, graceful, winding, stirring, rapid, or staccato rhythms?

Do you find conspicuous examples of unusual color combinations — unusual for their shapes, sizes, or kinds of color?

Are there any arrangements which remind you of some characteristics of the persons who made them?

Which do you find most attractive? Why?

A New Experiment

Choose three sheets of paper of different colors. Cut or tear each sheet into various geometric shapes, including one large piece, perhaps a triangle or a circle; some strips of various widths; and a number of small bits, such as circles or squares.

Select three sheets of paper — black, white, tan, or gray — for backgrounds. On each background place the largest piece of each color. Now choose some strips of different colors and place them on or near the large pieces, varying the colors. In this interchange, red, for example, may have green or yellow stripes on it; yellow, red and green stripes; green, red and yellow stripes. Distribute the smallest pieces either by scattering them over the entire arrangement or by grouping them in certain places in the design. Add any other pieces you like. Continue experimenting, until you have three very different arrangements.

Study the Results

1. Do you find that working experimentally, even with a few colors, you can create greatly varied color effects?
2. Does your work show planning and thought?
3. Does each arrangement really differ from the other two?
4. Notice how different the same colors appear when arranged on different backgrounds, in different proportions, and in different positions.

Have You Discovered That . . . ?

Colors change when used in different proportions?
Colors change when used in different positions?
Colors change with different backgrounds and neighbors?

Another Experiment: Texture

Make a collection of a wide variety of papers: rough, smooth, corrugated, perforated, sanded, and so on. Add bits of fabric interesting for their color and their *texture,* or surface quality, such as scrim, buckram, turkish toweling, flannel, gingham, and velvet. You may also make use of such contrasting materials as cork, lace, feathers, fur, fringe, buttons, shells, yarn, string, and cord.

Test Your New Materials

Make arrangements as you did before, enriching the variety of the combinations with interesting contrasts in texture.

While you experiment you may discover that colors, shapes, and textures suggest some object you know. A disk of green, red, or blue may remind you of a bush, an apple, or a lake. A brightly scalloped ribbon added here or there may suggest a circus tent, a parasol, or a scarf. Seen by an imaginative eye, sandpaper is swiftly transformed into a seashore, a garden path, or the roof of a barn; raveled yarn suggests a clown's wig, a bird's nest, or a caterpillar. Whatever you discover — and it should be your own discovery, one that has come from your own materials — build it up freely and with imagination, adding a variety of materials in an inventive way.

Remember that you are making a *decorative* design which aims primarily at pleasing the eye, rather than a *realistic* design which is concerned more with the way things actually appear.

Design with Color

Planning and organizing an arrangement lay the groundwork for design. Your arrangement may be either of familiar subjects or it may remain as an *abstract* design, that is, one without definite subject matter. In either case your concern is with the way in which the colors are brought together, the way they fill the background, and with the color rhythm of the whole design.

Decide on a satisfactory arrangement. Make it permanent by pinning, sewing, or pasting it to the background.

Study Your Work and That of the Class

1. Has color grown in power because:
   a. the development of a textural surface makes color richer and more pleasing?
   b. the color movement is better planned and therefore more rhythmic?
   c. the colors are more carefully selected and so take their place in the general color scheme?
2. Are these color arrangements more attractive, more striking, more original than your earlier ones?

Have You Discovered That . . . ?

Color takes on new power and new meaning when the texture is varied. Whether it is shiny or glistening, as we see it in metallic papers or in colored cellophane, ribbed or checked as in corrugated or in perforated paper, silky or woolly as in various fabrics, texture adds greatly to the quality of color. In good color groupings, varied textures add pleasing qualities to the whole arrangement.

Good organization in design produces harmony. Each part has a special place within the scheme of the whole design. The result of such organization within a design is called *unity*. When a design has unity it gives us a feeling of harmony and of beauty.

27

Look closely and you will see such things as a human profile on the right and a milkmaid on the left. Chagall, a modern artist, through a play of ideas and an unusual arrangement of them, makes this painting of a Russian village look like an illustration of a fairy tale.

This black and white reproduction of a painting reveals the flowing quality of its color. The artist has painted with such freedom that his subject may be interpreted in a number of ways; you may make your own choice.

29. I AND THE VILLAGE *Marc Chagall*

30. COMPOSITION WITH BIRD AND SHELLS *Isaac Muse*

Look for Color Enjoyment

Many fine examples of color can be found near at hand awaiting our recognition. Become color-conscious, and you will become aware of some of these examples. On your way to school or to work try to look for color in everything you see. Look at trees, skies, houses, and shops. Are you conscious of their color? You see people side by side in a subway and in the bus. Do you like the combinations of colors made by their costumes or would you like to change them and form new combinations? What about the colors on billboards, in magazines, and on packages that are to be seen everywhere? Can you quickly pick out the best in color? Such searching for color and attempting to evaluate its qualities are excellent aids in developing color judgment and color enjoyment.

Many books show the work of artists in color. Study both old and modern masters, particularly from the point of view of your knowledge of color.

Express Your Ideas in Words

Enjoyment comes not only through our observation and through our solution of problems, but also in learning to express our thoughts and feelings about all the things we see. If you make an effort to improve your art vocabulary, you will no longer find yourself saying, " I like it (or I don't like it), but I can't tell you why." Instead you may find yourself saying, " I like that design because I can feel its rhythm," or " If you took away some of the little spots from the corners, that design would have more unity."

Mix Your Own Colors

There is more power in a jar of paint or in a stick of chalk than you would imagine. Each color can be varied in a great number of ways. Whether you use chalk, or paint, or crayon, you are using a painting medium, one with which you can create color at will.

If you are to use chalks or crayons, see that they are clean and soft. Rubbed directly on the paper with strong, even strokes, they will give you clear, even color. You may mix colors by rubbing one over the other on the paper, then perhaps working them together with your finger tips.

If you are to use paints, select *opaque* colors, such as tempera or poster paints which, since they are not transparent, do not allow the paper to be seen through the color. These paints will serve you better at this time than water color which is transparent and requires experience for best results. The paint should be clean and creamy in consistency and — very important — the brush should be a large one. Use the paint directly from the jar or, if it comes in a tube, mix it with a little water on a clean palette, dish, or scrap of paper. Clean water and clean paint rags are important parts of your equipment.

Whatever color medium you use, take pride in keeping it in good condition and in using it as skillfully as possible.

Use Color to Understand It

Select three colors, or *hues,* and black and white. First try out the pure colors * on scrap paper, then try them out in experimental combinations and mixtures. Try using your colors in a variety of ways: sometimes let one color run into, and mix with, others directly on the paper. If you are using paints, try mixing them before putting them on the paper; then try applying other colors over the first ones in spots, in broken or wavy lines, or in any way that your imagination suggests.

Now take a large sheet of paper and without any preliminary drawing color the entire paper freely, working for a rich variety of color.

While Working . . .

Notice how colors change when you *add black, white, or other colors* to them. Some of them lose their original hues entirely. For example, orange and blue, when combined, produce brown. Other combinations, such as green and blue, when used together, produce a hue, blue-green, only slightly varied from each of its parts.

Notice that colors also change according to the *background* colors on which they are placed. For example, a bluish gray will appear blue against a gray background but gray against a blue background; a greenish yellow will seem green against a yellow ground and yellow against a green ground.

* Pure colors are the colors of the spectrum (see p. 33). They also are the colors of the rainbow, that is, red, orange, yellow, green, blue, and violet.

Here we find colors making a lively scene of a group of trees. Courageous painting, bold brush strokes, and the use of strong colors reveal the self-confidence of this young student of Argentina.

This modern Mexican artist captures the gaiety and movement of happy children. Imagination and observation, together with originality in color combinations, are his means of expressing a vivid scene.

31. ROSARIO, SANTA FE *Argentinian student*

32. CHILDREN'S PARTY *Jean Charlot*

Notice also how the qualities of lightness or darkness, the *values,* change in accordance with the color or colors near them. For example, orange will seem lighter against brown than against red; purple will seem darker against white than against black.

Notice how colors may appear brighter or duller, that is, how they gain or lose in *intensity* as you vary the colors near them. For example, yellow will appear brighter against dark blue than against red; red will appear brighter against green than against light brown.

Continue to Experiment

Make a new color variation, this time using as many colors as you wish. Try new color combinations and more unusual variations. Bring together, or *unify,* the whole experiment by repeating selected colors in various places. Try to emphasize a particular color by placing it in an important position; or by having it appear in a large amount; or by placing it against a color that makes it stand out; or by all three of these means.

Hold a Class Exhibition

Help to arrange an exhibition of the work of the entire class. First, look at the exhibition merely to enjoy it, to respond spontaneously to its color appeal. Then look at it a little more critically, more analytically, trying to answer these questions:

1. Are some arrangements more harmonious and pleasing than others?
2. Do some have more color movement, do they seem livelier, more rhythmic than others?
3. Do some arrangements fascinate you, stir your imagination?
4. Are you excited or amused by some; indifferent to others?
5. Is there one which seems to arouse in you very clearly a particular mood or a feeling; one that seems warm and gay, sunny and sparkling, bold and threatening, or depressing and dreary?
6. Can you analyze one of these arrangements? What qualities arouse in you a particular feeling? Is it the movement, the rhythm, the kind of color?
7. Do the colors themselves induce certain moods or emotions in you?

We have here two designs made directly, without any preliminary drawing. They show that it is possible to work as freely with colored papers as it is with paint. Whether the design is fantastic or amusing, the many combinations of color and the textures resulting from various treatments of the paper offer fascinating opportunities for inventive minds.

33. CUT PAPER *Student work*

34. CUT PAPER *Student work*

Have You Discovered That . . . ?

Colors can speak to us. They have a direct effect on our minds because we associate certain things with them. This is called *color association*. Whenever we see red, for example, we generally think of fire, of danger, of violent strife; red creates a stirring and emotional picture. Blue, on the other hand, calms, or perhaps even depresses. It has none of the challenging quality of red. What do the other colors mean to you?

Colors, then, are more than mere space fillers. If we open our eyes, if we are receptive, if our eyes are sensitive to color and conscious of it, we can realize the full meaning of what it has to say.

Color Speaks to and for You

Now that you have discovered that color can speak, use it to express your thoughts to others. First select colors that have definite meanings for you. There is a wide range from which you can select; some are gentle and quiet, others are dramatic and challenging. Use a definite color rhythm to convey a desired impression. Even the way in which color is applied — roughly or smoothly — can help to bring out your meaning or your mood.

More Facts for Your Grammar of Color

Now that you are beginning to study color as a language, it is time to examine your knowledge of its grammar, that is, its structure. This knowledge should help you to make color follow your will and to express your ideas clearly.

The paints used by artists are called *pigments*. Chemists make these pigments from many different substances. Pigments, whether water colors, oils, crayons, or pastels, are made up in colors as true to those in the *spectrum* as possible. The spectrum is an image formed when a light ray is separated into its pure colors by refraction through a prism. If we hold a prism up to the sunlight, we see the pure colors of the spectrum as they appear in the rainbow. The student of physics speaks of color in terms of light rays, the psychologist, in terms of color sensations, while the artist considers it in terms of pigment.

Pigments are not always as brilliant as the spectrum colors, and therefore some of the color theories of the scientist cannot be directly applied by the artist. He develops his own theories through his observation and through his own experience in using pigments. Because the artist is dependent upon the chemist for his colors, he accepts the three colors, red, yellow, and blue as *primary* colors. These are called primary colors because all the other colors are made by mixing these three in varying proportions. To obtain secondary colors, he mixes red with yellow to produce orange, yellow with blue for green, red with blue for violet or for purple. We suggest that you experiment with colors in order that you may become acquainted with their various qualities.

Study the Fundamental Colors

Paint small areas of the three primary colors, red, blue, and yellow, on paper. Mix and apply similar areas of orange, green, and violet to the paper. You will now have six colors, or *hues:* red, orange, yellow, green, blue, and violet. The term hue is used to differentiate one color from another; for instance, blue from green, yellow from red. These six hues should be as strong and as pure as possible. The word intensity or *chroma,* indicates the degree of color strength or saturation which can range from full, rich color to grayed or neutral tones.

Now try to produce a wide range in other mixtures of colors. Use black and white as two additional hues to mix with your primary colors. Choose one color, let us say red, and mix as many different kinds of red as possible. Use the following suggestions:

1. Add varying amounts of orange to red and paint small areas of each mixture on a sheet of paper.
2. Add violet in gradually increasing amounts and paint each mixture you have made on the same paper.
3. Repeat the same experiment using white as the color added to red.
4. Repeat the experiment using black in varying amounts.

It will be interesting to study this single sheet of paper with all the samples of red you have painted. You will see how many variations of one hue are possible. Answer these questions:

1. How many different kinds of red did you produce?
2. Did you obtain light reds, orange reds, violet reds, and intermediate tones of all these hues?

34

Further Experimentation

Now take the other two primary colors, yellow and blue, and experiment with them as you did with red. Following that, experiment by mixing various hues to find the best way of obtaining subdued, or less intense colors. Study your results, then answer the following questions:

1. Did you mix colors that seem to be most contrasting to each other, such as yellow and violet, red and green, orange and blue, to obtain neutral tones?
2. Can you name or describe each color you have mixed? Could you say, for example, that one was a pale, bluish green; that another was a salmon pink?
3. In mixing, did you use equal amounts of each color? If so, try using a very small amount of one color and notice how different is the effect on the other color.

Analyze Color

Every object we look at has color. Try to analyze all colors, or hues, around you. The term *hue* is used to distinguish one color from another. In distinguishing between light and dark colors we refer to that property of color known as *value;* in distinguishing between bright and dull colors we refer to that property of color known as *intensity* (see p. 31). The three properties of color — hue, value, and intensity — are part of the vocabulary of color theory in pigments.

Often the commercial names of colors give no indication of how they have been obtained or mixed. Try to imagine yourself mixing a paint to be called Nile Green. Would you use a little blue with the green, some white, and possibly a touch of red? If so, then Nile Green is actually a light, subdued, bluish green.

Remember that only by constant practice can you learn to observe colors, and that experience in making mixtures and using them in combinations is a surer way to gain confidence in the use of color than by following many rules.

What Have You Learned?

Assemble all your previous experiments. Spread them out so that you may see each one clearly. This little one-man show records your development from the first plunge into color to your more controlled use of it. Do you see definite evidences of your improvement? Try checking them by this list:

1. Have you shown courage in the use of color; kept away from your own favorites; tested all kinds of color?
2. Is your use of color becoming more original and personal?
3. Does your work show that you are becoming increasingly able to think and work by yourself?
4. Have you used materials with increasing power and boldness?
5. Can you feel a growing power to express yourself both freely and harmoniously in color?
6. Have you used your knowledge of the grammar of color to good effect?

Here are a few questions about *you*, the person who is responsible for this exhibition. What has happened to you during the time you have been exploring color? Do you find that you are now more interested in color than you were before, that you enjoy and appreciate it more? Do you wish now to revolutionize your color world, to change the walls, to repaint the landscape, and to dramatize yourself through color? Have you become interested in making yourself a person of good judgment and good taste?

If so, it is now time for you to investigate the part color plays in the world about you. This means not only the world of art, but also the world of everyday things.

4.
THE THEATER

THE SHOWMAN or the stage designer who organizes a spectacle knows that it is his problem to gain and to hold the attention of the spectators. He seeks to lift them from the realm of everyday life into a make-believe world which they can, for the time, believe true. He also knows that color is his most powerful instrument in accomplishing this end, for color is the language understood by every audience. Cleverly he sets his stage, constantly using color, suggestive, exciting color that, like a chariot, magically transports us to an unfamiliar and fascinating world.

The stage designer studies color thoroughly for the stage setting, for the costumes, the properties, and the lighting of his production. He considers every subtlety, every possible meaning and effect that it could have on his audience. He knows that there are endless ways to use color in stage design; that it is impossible to exhaust the inventiveness and the ingenuity of the human mind in searching for ways to delight, to startle, or to fascinate. We realize this since color has been added to the movies. At first the motion-picture people were satisfied just to reproduce colors. Then, through experimentation, they learned how to control color so that the great possibilities for thus enriching motion pictures are being realized.

Color Has Many Uses

Actor's makeup is only a small part of the color used to create the illusion desired. An actor's costume, in its design, its texture, and its color, is carefully considered to strengthen his characterization and make him part of the color mood of the whole play. The use of all kinds of colored lights, with their power to transform color and shape, to blend or to intensify them, to make them whisper or shout, can create from cardboard and tinsel a world of apparent reality. To the audience the stage designer can present bright morning or gloomy night; warmth of tropics or freezing cold; aching suspense or riotous gaiety.

The Magic Wand

A trip backstage astonishes us. We touch a bit of cotton, or oilcloth, or crudely painted cardboard, and find it hard to believe that we saw these things as an ermine robe, rich tapestry, a moss-bound castle wall. How was it possible to create these illusions from ordinary materials? Was it really true that the ghost did not emerge from a closet but was standing on the stage all the time, concealed behind a shadow? Certainly we saw a sword go right through the villain's back, but here he is, alive and unharmed. The golden-haired princess removes her braids, and we find her no longer a romantic and lovely picture. This is the magic we love. Like all magic tricks they appear simple as soon as we understand how they are produced. The materials are commonplace, yet the illusion is complete.

What is this magic that the stage designer has at his command? How is he able to sweep his audience into any mood; to create at will the illusions of time, of place, and of space? What is its relation to art?

A Make-believe World

Even in miniature, the world of make-believe seems real. The doll house your little sister plays with, the fort your small brother builds of sand or of snow, are both transformed by imagination into a part of the real world. In the same way a small box can become a stage on which ideas may take shape. The professional stage designer often begins by working with a miniature stage just as you are now about to do.

You will see how color can be made to work for a definite purpose. From first to last, allow your imagination free play.

Build Your Stage

To build a stage take a box that is about nine inches wide and twelve inches long. Cut away one of its long sides. Stand it upright on the other long side which then becomes the floor of the stage. The back and sides of

38

The menace of the jungle is dramatized in this scene by one huge tree and one tiny figure. The tree might be made of cardboard and painted muslin might be used to suggest the sky, yet with these simple means an illusion is created. What colors do you think the artist used to convey the desired mood?

35. EMPEROR JONES   *Cleon Throckmorton*

36. DON JUAN AND FAUST   *Hans Wilderman*

To symbolize the meaning of the Faust legend, man's search for truth and happiness, the artist designed an abstract stage setting that helps the actors develop their theme.

39

the box form the background and side walls of the stage. The open top allows for arrangement of materials. The open front is the *proscenium,* or front-of-stage opening. Paint the outside of the box black. Now you have a stage.

Start with the Backdrop

Select chalks, paints, or colored papers. On nine-by-twelve inch paper experiment with colors in order to create various moods. Use scrap materials, colored papers, solid and transparent fabrics, in addition to paint and chalk, since a wise use of textural contrasts will heighten the effect you wish to produce. Make several trial sheets for your background, working until you have one that is really individual and imaginative.

Test the trial sheets within your stage to judge the results. Decide which seems most dramatic in its expression of a mood whether gay or sinister, warlike or peaceful, happy or tragic. Choose the one that appeals to you most vividly and leave it temporarily within your stage. Now cover the floor and the sides of the stage, considering color and texture in relation to the backdrop.

Analyze Your Results

1. What mood have you caught? Does it suggest a particular time, place, or condition, such as early morning or late afternoon, sky or ocean, fire or storm?
2. Does your color produce an emotional state, such as fear, hope, depression, serenity, or excitement? Has it qualities of an unearthly or a supernatural kind?
3. Do you think that the mood or emotional effect may be quickly caught by the audience?

Add to Your Idea

This mood now becomes the central theme of your stage setting. Study it carefully to see what new ideas it gives you. Just as in your early experiments in color you found suggestions of recognizable things in your design, so here your imagination can find and bring to life similar suggestions. A bit of color in the backdrop may bring to mind a church spire, a boat, or an

3. A color varies in its appearance according to the colors used with it. It will appear warmer or cooler, brighter or duller, lighter or darker, according to the kind, the amount, the proportion, the values, and the intensities of the colors that are near it. Therefore no color can be chosen without testing it in relation to the general color scheme. Thus, after thinking that you need a certain color, let us say green, in your color scheme, it will be necessary for you to try out several different kinds of greens, such as light and dark greens, bright and dull greens, warm and cool greens, in varying amounts and in varying places. Only after such experiments can you really be sure of having found a final solution to your color problem.

Now for the Actors

No stage setting seems complete without actors. Can you think of the characters that should belong to this creation of yours and play a part in it? Do you need a hero and a heroine, and possibly a villain?

Construct figures to represent the characters you have thought of; use any materials, such as plasticine, pipe cleaners, wire, tiny boxes, and similar odds and ends. Work for an expressive shape, remembering that exaggeration helps to characterize a figure and give it personality. Long, or thin, or wide, or squat shapes are all related in our minds to certain types of people. Each character should fit the mood of your stage setting and should be definite in type, such as dynamic, menacing, ethereal, graceful, or fantastic.

When you are satisfied with the characterization of the figure, complete it with whatever color you think advisable both to help define the figure and its place in the play, and to make it harmonious with the scene.

Complete the Scene

The things that supplement the action on the stage, such as furniture, are called properties. Add the properties you think may be needed, remembering to keep them in scale with the actors.

Construct your stage set carefully, and make sure that it can be moved without falling apart or having the figures within it displaced. Work in a careful, craftsmanlike way.

Judge and Jury

Plan to hold an exhibition of class work. Analyze, compare, judge the results. Answer the following questions about the exhibits:

1. Which seems most complete in its organization and its use of harmonious color?
2. Which has made exceptionally good use of a knowledge of color?
3. Which shows the greatest originality in ideas?
4. Which shows the greatest inventiveness in the use of materials?
5. Which is the most expressive and dramatic?
6. Which has caught an unusual mood?

Now that you know something of stage designing you will doubtless feel better prepared to judge the work of professional designers who have made significant contributions to this field. You may also find school and club productions a challenge to your creative abilities as a stage designer.

40. LUTE SONG *Robert Edmond Jones*

In this design for a stage setting of a Chinese play, a famous American designer has used a starkly neutral background to intensify the delicate charm of the figure in pink.

41. KING LEAR *Norman Bel Geddes*

Here warm, glowing color has been used freely and dramatically against large areas of somber color. Notice how the repetition of colors heightens both the rhythmic and the emotional quality of the scene.

5.
PAINTING

WE HAVE SEEN that color can speak directly to us. It can define shapes, reveal masses, and suggest forms. Color can soothe, irritate, challenge, excite. It can be rich, harmonious, glowing, or weak. That is why color is so stimulating to painters and why it serves as their most direct instrument in expressing what they wish to say.

When we watch a painter at work, we see that he generally uses color as the starting point for his work. Read what some famous artists have written about the way they saw color and how they reacted to it. Vincent Van Gogh, the Dutch painter wrote:

"This time it is simply my bedroom. Only color can express it and through simplification give it greater style and create an atmosphere of rest and sleep. The walls are a light violet, the floor has a pattern of red boards. The wooden bed is as yellow as fresh butter, the curtain, the cover and the pillow are lemon yellow and green and very light. The bedspread, scarlet red and the window, green.

"The washbasin is orange in color, the pitcher blue, the doors lavender, and that is all; otherwise there is nothing in this room.

"The square furniture must give an expression of unshakable quiet.

"The frame of the picture will be white, as there is no white in the picture. That balances the enforced quiet that I wished to express."

(from "Letters to His Brother")

Henri Matisse, the French painter, wrote:

"Suppose I set out to paint an interior: I have before me a cupboard; it gives me a sensation of bright red; I put down a red which satisfies me;

immediately a relation is established between this red and the white of the canvas. If I put a green near the red, if I paint in a yellow floor, there must still be between this green, this yellow and the white of the canvas a relation that will be satisfactory to me."

(from " La Grande Revue, Dec., 1908)

Do quotations like these help you to understand that each painter speaks and reveals himself through the language of color? Those of us who possess color vision are able to find great satisfaction and enjoyment in making color a part of our lives.

Painting Is a Symphony in Color

When we listen to a symphony, we feel emotion and enjoyment. We know that the composer needs great creative power in order to obtain harmony, tonal quality in sound, and originality of theme. Although the composer and the painter work in very different media, the effects of a great painting and a stirring symphony are very similar. In each there is a weaving together of numberless tones or colors. The more complete the meaning, the pattern, the color, and the movement of a painting, the more certain we can be that the artist used all his creative ability to create a harmonious whole.

The Old Habit

Many of us have set color ideas when we recall certain familiar objects. We have only to hear the word rose and the color red is most likely to come to mind. Just so the word sky brings blue to our minds, trees are generally thought of as green, and clouds white. It is almost as automatic as the way the typewriter works when we strike a key. We must learn to avoid this weakness, this automatic reaction to specific colors.

Do you remember the days when you were very young and used color with great abandon? When skies were pink and houses purple; when cows might be blue and elephants pink? Then you did not select colors automatically or with a prejudiced mind; you chose them freely. Those of us who can carry over from our childhood a fine and independent color sense are well on the way to using color creatively.

42. TAHITIAN LANDSCAPE WITH PEACOCKS *Paul Gauguin*

Gauguin, the French artist, used rich and riotous color to portray the beauty of the tropical scene around him. This painting shows how much he loved color and how greatly he enjoyed using it in a flat, decorative pattern. Gauguin's skies might be pink or his mountains yellow, for he used color to please his eye rather than to imitate nature.

Chart a New Color Course

Let us begin by opening our eyes on this rich world of color which is constantly changing not only in hue but also in value and intensity. How wide a range of color between the drab street corner and the gay shopping district; the sandy beach and the gaily dressed bathers, the colored lights and the gay costumes of a circus and the dull interior of an old railroad station! We have only to look around us to realize the infinite variety of color to be found in nature. Even the smallest of her creations, flowers, butterflies, insects, caterpillars, shells, when closely examined, show astonishing richness of color.

It should not be hard to understand why the painter, who is so sensitive to color and so aware of it, uses it to express his thoughts. For him there is no familiar recipe of " roses are red and violets blue." He does more than recognize color; he sees it as he wishes to see it, or as he needs to see it, or simply as he feels it. Whether he is developing or dramatizing a scene, creating an atmosphere or a mood, revealing a personality or describing a crowd, color is his servant, not his master.

Color Media

Painters work with many different color media, such as oil paint, water color, fresco, tempera, chalks, and crayons. Each medium, because of its specific qualities, fulfills the particular purpose for which it is best suited. Thus we use oil paints for a prolonged study, water color for a quick, vivid impression, fresco for a permanent wall painting. In the hands of an experienced artist, however, each medium becomes an individual tool suited to his personality, his particular interests, his ideas, and his needs.

Time for Action

Undoubtedly you have all painted as a pastime, instinctively but with incomplete knowledge. Now it is time to begin painting again, this time to gain knowledge. We know you will enjoy this experience.

In order that color may speak for you as directly as possible, we suggest that you choose a simple color medium such as tempera, chalk, or crayon. Thus you will avoid the difficulties of involved techniques with media that require longer study and definite control.

That this nineteenth-century artist had a sympathetic understanding of the lives of some of his contemporaries is shown by his portrayal of them in their humble and everyday surroundings. The beauty of this painting lies in the boldly silhouetted figures of the mother and her child, and in its deep, dramatic tones.

This is a theme of movement, of people, of brilliant lights and moving shadows. Nash, a modern English painter, has caught its spirit through the use of rhythmic lines, of strongly defined areas, and of a bold lively brush treatment.

43. THE LAUNDRESS *Honoré Daumier*

44. WASH LINE *Tom Nash*

Check Your Materials

If you use paints for your first experience, see that you have, as a minimum, red, yellow, blue, black, and white. These paints should be creamy in consistency. You will also need a large brush, a jar of water, paper at least twelve by eight inches in size, and scrap paper.

If you use chalks or crayons, see that they are clean, soft, and varied in color. You should have both large paper and scrap paper.

Directions for Their Use

If your medium is paint, you must use a great deal of color in order to have free, bold, and effective painting. Fill your brush constantly; keep it loaded with paint. Wash your brush each time you use a new color to avoid muddiness. Colors may be mixed on a palette or on a scrap of paper.

If chalk or crayon is your medium, hold the stick flat on its side and use it in broad, sweeping strokes. Mix colors directly on the paper as you did before. If you like a smooth effect, rub them with your fingers or a bit of cloth.

Stir Your Imagination

Do not make a pencil drawing first. Begin by using colors at random. Mix and combine them to cover the whole sheet of paper. It is better to let colors shade or run into one another than to fill in a definite outline.

Use the colors in a variety of ways. They may be flat and smooth; they may appear in strokes, in bold waves, or in broken or rough spots. Shade some from light to dark or from bright to dull; break up others by placing lines or spots of other colors over them. In this way you can give the effect of different textures and thus, as you know, add a new attraction to the color.

Let Color Speak to You

Study your work from a distance. Turn it around in order to see it in all possible positions. This will help you to find the angle from which the color seems to have most movement.

Examine your work intently. Can you find some lines or some colors that suggest to you a definite movement or action? If so, study them and try to analyze their characteristics. Can you imagine or perhaps see in them some suggestion as definite as galloping horses; children running through a storm; a hurricane; a flood; or an explosion? Perhaps something suggests a sleeping figure, a skyscraper, a locomotive, or a sailboat. You might even find a palm tree in the desert, or icebergs under an Arctic sun.

Whatever you discover, make use of it as a suggestion for a new painting. Let this suggestion start ideas. Consider how these ideas can develop into definite shapes, how they can be made to resemble, as imaginatively as you wish, people, places, and things.

Summon a Painting Mood

With your first painting experiment before you as a guide, begin a new painting on fresh paper. Use the ideas you gathered from your earlier effort and make them recognizable. Fill the paper with other things related to your newly found subject.

Feel what you paint and make your color express what you feel. Color and movement suggest figures and objects and can make them seem more real than any details possibly could. Therefore, strive to paint the essence, the heart of your subject, not its outer covering. For example, the figure of a child running through a storm can be beautifully expressed by the movement of color and of line. Such details as facial expression or buttons on a coat are not necessary; in fact, they detract from the vividness of the figure.

Make your color meaningful and dramatic. Remember not to limit it to conventional color recipes such as brown for tree trunks, blue for the sky, white for a sail. Use such colors only when you need them for your color scheme or to emphasize, to contrast, or to repeat other colors.

Now Judge Your Results

1. Have you used your paint or chalk in a fluid, broad, free way?
2. Does your work show confidence in your own ideas?
3. Are your ideas original, inventive, entirely your own?
4. Have you used color to build up your ideas and to create an interest in them?
5. Is there rich variety in the kind and quality of color used?
6. Did you use light and dark, bright and dull contrasts in color?
7. Is the whole color effect pleasing and harmonious?

A profoundly religious spirit is characteristic of the work of this modern French painter. Seldom do we find richer and more emotionally moving color. It has often been compared to that of stained glass.

Paintings by this challenging and highly original Spanish artist show his tireless interest in experimentation and his search for a new form of expression. This study is composed of interesting objects which have been interpreted in the artist's individual way.

45. THE OLD KING *Georges Roualt*

46. STILL LIFE WITH BLACK BUST *Pablo Picasso*

47. GUIDO DA FOGLIANO *Simone Martini*

A striking portrait of a nobleman reveals through its angular lines and its
bold geometric pattern the artist's feeling for design. This Italian painter
of the early fourteenth century made use of the pageantry of his time.

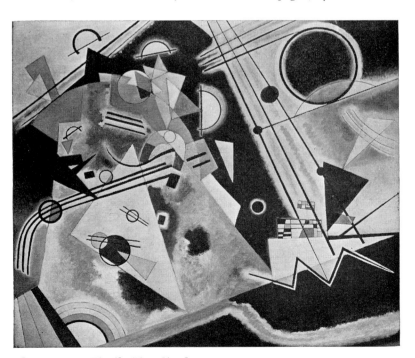

48. SERENE *Vasily Kandinsky*

Kandinsky, a modern Russian artist, used geometric shapes to suggest and
to interpret a mood. In this painting we find a highly organized and intricate interweaving of lines, of shapes, and of colors.

49. BUFFALO HUNTER *Early American artist*

This dramatic picture was painted by an unknown and evidently self-trained artist. The vividness of the scene and his interest in dramatic action were sufficient to inspire a painting for which he relied entirely on his own memory and imagination.

50. ZAPATISTOS *José Orozco*

A painter close to the hearts of his people usually portrays them in a simple and direct way. This modern Mexican artist expresses a social movement with primary color and through a simple and vigorous treatment.

8. If you were to repaint your subject, which parts would you keep and which would you try to improve?

A painting, to be successful as a whole, must be well organized. The organization of a painting is known as its *composition*.

Composition in a Painting

A *composition* is a unified arrangement of lines, masses, and colors. You have been using these elements to express your ideas. Certain facts concerning their use will be helpful in your future work.

1. A composition should have a center of attraction which acts as a force to hold all the parts together. The center of attraction may be brought out, or emphasized, in a variety of ways.
   a. It may be very large.
   b. It may be very light.
   c. It may be very dark.
   d. It may be very bright.
   e. It may be strongly contrasted with other colors.
   f. It may be the area to which lines or color movements lead.
   g. It may be brought out by a combination of the foregoing means.
2. A composition should have balance. Balance may be achieved through:
   a. Distribution of different kinds, amounts and qualities of color;
   b. Distribution of light and dark or of small and large masses;
   c. Organization of line and color movement.

There is a wide range of possibility in the combinations of these means. It ranges from even, formal, or symmetrical, to uneven, informal, asymmetrical balance of colors, of masses, and of lines.

Assemble Your Work

Take your previous experiments and arrange them in the order in which you made them. Compare your first and your last pieces of work. Analyze them for color composition, for balance, and for emphasis. Consider how you might improve your compositions if you were to repeat them.

Do you find marked differences between your first effort and your last? Does the latter show that you gained greatly in understanding and in use of color; that you now have more power to express your ideas through color; that you have more control over your materials?

Are you eager for more painting, and ready to experiment with color in other ways?

Memory Speaks

We need not travel over all the earth to find exciting subjects to paint. The way we see things in their own familiar surroundings can make them more vivid, more exciting than any subject with which we are not personally familiar. If you are observant, you will store in your memory daily a number of impressions. The same little porch, the same street corner, or sand lot will impress each of you differently. The familiar pile of books, umbrellas, and rubbers seen by you and your classmates may give widely varying impressions to each of you.

The coffeepot, the kitchen sink, the view from your back window may not seem fascinating or beautiful in themselves at first glance, yet artists have made use of similar subjects in paintings that are as exciting and as stirring as scenes of strange lands and people. A familiar, commonplace subject may be beautiful when the artist has enough vision to make it so.

Memory Is a Point of Departure

Recall a recent vivid scene, an experience, or an impression such as a snowstorm in the morning, umbrellas at the beach, backyard wash lines, Saturday-night shopping. What do you remember most clearly? Can you recall some color movement, some conspicuous lines of action that might serve now as a starting point for a composition? Will your mental picture lend itself to broad and free color treatment?

Let your mind dwell on the remembered scene until you can see it vividly in terms of color. Which colors will best interpret its character and mood, lively and gay, dull and somber, or mysterious and weird?

How to Begin

Select a color for a background paper which you think is the most suggestive for the scene you have in mind, such as black for night, yellow for the seashore, lavender for snow.

54

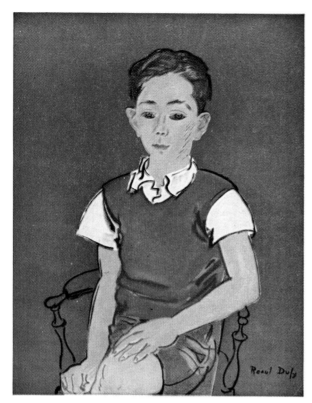

Dufy, a modern French artist, has painted the portrait of a young boy with colors that bring out the model's youth and vitality. The warm skin tones are brilliant against the contrasting blue of the background. Strong, simple lines and sensitive placing of the figure make it a beautiful and appealing design.

51. PORTRAIT OF MICHEL *Raoul Dufy*

Notice how a great master simplifies drawing and detail so that only the most important elements of his subject are included. Matisse, a modern French artist, created a rich, tapestry-like pattern with rhythmically repeated colors.

52. RECLINING WOMAN *Henri Matisse*

Now choose the colors that will interpret your theme well. Test them on the back of the paper to see if they need to be made lighter or darker. Without any preliminary drawing, paint directly on the paper the most important color masses. Add the less important, considering the various methods you know that will emphasize a center of attraction.

When you work, use your color in various ways, at times smoothly, again, roughly. Use broken lines and irregular spots of color; vary the textures. Instead of covering the whole background with color, use some of it as a part of your design.

Watch While You Work

Check your work for the following requirements:

1. The color should remain fresh and clean.
2. It should express the mood of your subject.
3. It must have a center of attraction.
4. The composition must be balanced through the distribution of color and of masses, and through organization of line directions.
5. The picture must have enough meaning to make it seem complete.

Keep on Painting

First attempts at painting are seldom completely successful from the point of view of art, but they are valuable as a testing ground for your control of the materials and the development of your ideas.

After analyzing your first experiment, make a second attempt, using either the same subject or one totally different. Work systematically to overcome previous weaknesses. If you find that your memory of a scene or an object is not perfectly clear, go, if possible, to the place where you saw it in order to study what you now find is not clear to you.

Now that you have made some compositions from memory, your judgment should be better and you should have a greater understanding of your problem. You should be more discriminating and better able to select important lines, masses, and colors when working from an actual model. Your eye must see, your mind judge and select, and finally, your hand must record the most expressive, the most challenging aspect of your subject.

Close Attention Is Needed

Use your background of color experiences, your imagination, and, above all, a sharp and keen eye when you observe people, places, and things. Look at them as a painter does. See dramatically, vividly, colorfully. Keep your eyes open for characteristic lines and shapes, for striking patterns and textures. Be sensitive to color qualities and to color relations.

Choose a Subject

Choose one of your classmates who, because of his costume or other striking color contrasts, would make a good subject for a painting. Pose the model in a place where the class can see his whole figure, either front or side view.

How to See Your Model

Look at the entire figure for vertical, angular, curved, and horizontal line directions. These basic lines reveal the pose and the structure of the figure. Try to see the relative proportions of head, torso, arms, and legs.

Observe carefully the physical characteristics of the model, noting such things as long or round head; thin, fat, long, or short neck; broad or narrow shoulders; stocky or slender figure.

Put It Down on Paper

Try to see the figure as though drawn on paper. It should be so placed that it fills the paper well, that is, neither too small nor too large for the paper.

Use either thin, light-colored paint or chalk to block in the main lines and the relative proportions of the figure. Try to avoid the common error of making the lower part of the figure too small for the upper part. Try also to see the true proportions of the hands and the feet, for here again the average person makes them too small.

Keep on looking at the model as you work. Improve your first attempt by going over it with a slightly darker color. Do not worry if the first colors extend beyond the corrections, for in your final painting you will cover all your first work.

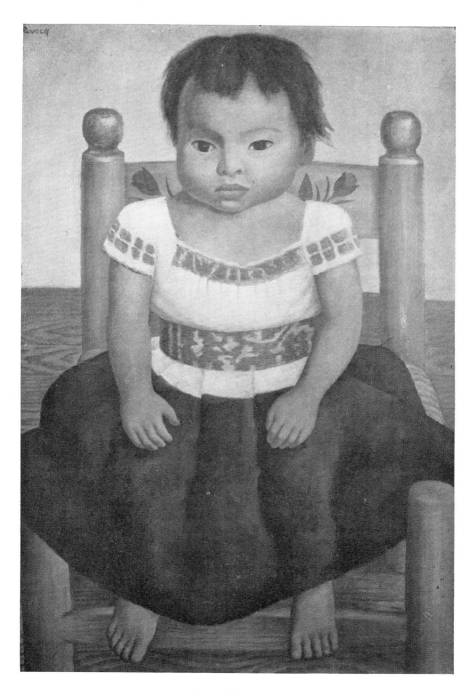

53. PORTRAIT OF MODESTA *Diego Rivera*

How well this modern Mexican artist understands the art of portraying a child!
Large, dark eyes, solid little body, and small hands and feet make their appeal, and
the simple treatment is in keeping with the spirit of the child.

57

54. BABY IN RED CHAIR *Early American artist*

An early American craftsman and sign painter, who made portrait painting a part of
his trade, shows keen observation and a wonderful sense of humor in his treatment of
this smiling baby.

58

55. PORTRAIT OF A YOUTH *Pinturicchio*

In this painting by an Italian of the sixteenth century we find a dignified and beautifully composed figure placed in fine relationship to the spacious Italian landscape. Paintings such as this will always be understood and enjoyed.

56. QUEEN ISABELLA *Diego Velásquez*

Remarkable observation and a high degree of skill, combined with an astute understanding of the character of his models, make the portraits of Velásquez outstanding. This seventeenth-century Spanish artist enjoyed painting textural variety such as we see in this queenly costume.

Now the Real Painting Begins

When you are satisfied with your preliminary interpretation of the figure, you are ready to build it up. Observe the model carefully for color, noting the main color differences of flesh, of hair, and of costume. Mix colors to approximate those you see.

Now try to emphasize the character and the color of each individual part of the figure. Use flat, broken, or shaded color, whatever you like. While painting, do not stop for unimportant details, such as the features of the face, patterns in necktie or dress, buttons, or shoelaces.

Include a Background and a Floor

On scrap paper make trials in color for a background. These colors need not be the exact colors you see; they may be selected by you because you think they would be an improvement over what you actually see. Keep in mind that they are a part of the color composition and must contribute to it. Hold each trial against the painted figure to see if it will bring out the figure clearly. Remember that some colors seem to recede, thus giving a feeling of depth, while others seem to advance, giving an impression of being very near the spectator. If you are not satisfied with your color trials, make them lighter, darker, brighter, duller, warmer, cooler, until you find the background color that presents the painted figure to advantage.

In like manner plan the color for the floor, choosing one you think goes well with those you have already used. The color of the floor, however, should not be as strong a contrast to the figure as is the background. Since the lower part of the figure is less important, it should not be over-emphasized.

Paint in the colors that you have selected. Make any changes needed in the structure and the color of the figure to bring it out with emphasis.

Arrange an Exhibition

1. Pin up the work of the entire class and compare one painting with another.
2. Vote for the most successful painting and be prepared to give the reasons for your choice.
3. Consider your own painting critically. Decide which parts of the figure you observed most keenly and which parts need further study.

4. Determine the most successful parts of your painting from the standpoint of color expression.

The World about You

Look about you for other interesting subjects. You might like to paint a head or a group of figures as seen from your window. A corner of your bedroom, a plant, some colorful objects on the table may inspire you.

Learn to look at your subject again and again until you know its characteristics well enough to paint it. Simple or complicated, familiar or strikingly new, the subject is only the point of departure. The way in which you see it and your interpretation of it are what give your painting originality.

After you have painted, you are better prepared to study the paintings of an artist, to understand and enjoy them. Since you understand some of the problems of painting through your own personal experience, you are better able to understand the artist himself, his aims, his ideas, and his individuality, as revealed in his work.

Look for Paintings

Visit the museums and become familiar with their collections of paintings. Visit libraries, galleries, and shops that exhibit paintings. Find reproductions of paintings in books, in catalogs, in magazines, and in newspapers.

Things to Consider in Looking at Paintings

Have you seen paintings, heretofore unfamiliar, that impress you as being striking, or challenging, or worth studying? If so, first of all, let the painting itself speak to you. Give yourself time to take in its particular appeal, to analyze it, study carefully its particular message, its style, its contribution to the field of color, its manner of expression, or technique. A check list, such as the one that follows, is invaluable in analyzing a painting, in helping you to find definite reasons for your appreciation and your enjoyment of it.

1. Does the artist paint things exactly as they look or does he give a personal interpretation to his subject?

In tempera paint this South American artist has created a striking composition of three forceful figures. They are painted with the same solidity that we find in the illustration below. In addition, the strong, line movements suggest action even in the resting figures.

Objects as commonplace as eggs have been treated in an expressive way in this painting. The solid forms are placed in careful relationship and give an effect of quiet repose.

57. STEVEDORES RESTING *Alfredo Guido*

58. EGGS *Maurice Grosser*

59. KRISHNA QUELLING KALIYA *Indian Rajput, XVIII cent.*

In this painting the artist has chosen a mythological theme, a hero slaying the serpent Kaliya while the wives of the monster plead for his life. The strong pattern of dark and light adds to the exciting action of the scene.

Even sand may be a painting medium. Various colors, trickled through the fingers of a craftsman, formed this symbolic and rhythmical picture.

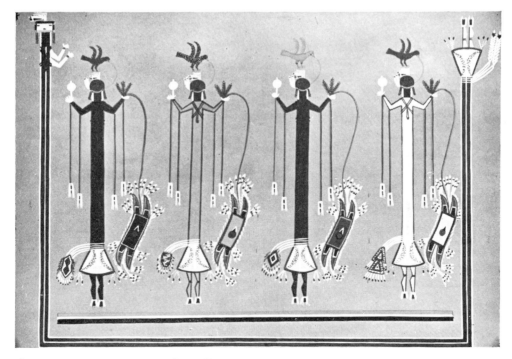

60. SAND PAINTING *Navajo Indian*

61. SLEEPING GYPSY *Henri Rousseau*

A self-trained French painter of the late nineteenth century composed this fantastic and highly original scene. The lion, the moon, and the sleeping figure with his guitar cannot help but stir our imagination.

A love of fantasy is shown by this modern Brazilian artist in creating this unreal and lively scene. The scarecrow is a dominating figure in the forceful pattern of dark and light. We are conscious of brilliant light, of great space, and even of the breeze which seems to bring the scarecrow to life.

62. SCARECROW *Cândido Portinari*

63. THE ANNUNCIATION   *Fra Angelico*

Fra Angelico, an Italian painter of the thirteenth century, achieved a
deeply touching and spiritual quality in this painting which he placed on
the walls of his monastery.

Mosaics, made from bits of colored stone, were designed as wall decorations and were widely used in the early Christian era. This typically religious subject is presented with dignity and reverence.

64. THE GOOD SHEPHERD   *Early Italian*

65. DESCENT FROM THE CROSS *Giotto*

A late thirteenth-century painter, Giotto, is considered one of the greatest masters of all time. He has painted this religious subject with great devotion. Notice the restrained poses of the figures.

Religious subjects were always the theme of early Italian paintings. However, each artist interpreted his chosen theme in his own way. Da Fabriano made the most of jeweled and decorated costumes. Notice the feeling of movement achieved by the arrangement of figures and of light shapes.

66. ADORATION OF THE MAGI *Gentile da Fabriano*

2. Does the artist paint in order to tell a story or to further a cause?
3. Is his interpretation of his subject unusual, challenging, dramatic, inspiring?
4. Does the color in the painting help to create the mood, the atmosphere, or the action?
5. Can you connect the color treatment with your own color experiences?
6. Would you like to have this painting or a reproduction of it in your room for further study and enjoyment?

Enrich Your Background

In addition to looking at paintings, you may learn something of the various forms of this art by reading books about paintings and painters. In this way you will realize how paintings not only express the artist but also represent the period in which he worked. The more you know about each particular historical art period, the customs, the manner of living, the outstanding events, economic and political, the spiritual life, and main interests of the times, the better equipped you will be to evaluate the true spirit of the paintings of that period. A study of the history of art will acquaint you with the different types of painting throughout the ages: *religious* painting, inspired by the content of religion; *secular* painting, concerned with things of the physical world; *genre* painting, depicting immediate, everyday life. It will explain to you how these types developed from the spiritual life or the interests and needs of the people of that time.

Make a report on an artist in whose work you are interested, including a summary of his life and his time. Give your report orally to the class, illustrating it, if possible, with reproductions of his work.

Be Open-minded

Have your own experiences and observations proved to you by this time that painting is a fluid, everchanging, and highly personal expression of thought and of feeling? Be alert to its developments as they appear in your own generation and become a part of it. Through personal discovery of both modern and traditional painting you will gain greatly in understanding and in enjoyment of this timeless art.

67. POSTER *E. McKnight Kauffer*

Gay colors and a charming, childlike quality of design are used by this American poster artist to make even a subway trip in England seem attractive.

6.
ADVERTISING

WHEN WE HAVE a product to sell or a message to convey, we immediately think of advertising as one of the best ways of reaching people. There are many ways to advertise, but only those which are in the art field concern us here, and the poster is one of these.

Posters need power. The poster artist knows that he must design his poster so that it will catch and hold the attention of the spectator long enough to convey a message. A striking design is necessary because the poster must combat public indifference, compete with moving objects, with lights, and with all the distracting things that are found in crowded places.

Color is, of course, the most direct agent in helping the poster quickly and vividly to broadcast its message. Therefore, the main requirement of a poster is vigorous treatment, consisting of striking color areas and brilliant contrasts of light and dark to emphasize the center of attraction. A brief, well-worded message is highly important and the lettering used to convey it should be bold, strong in contrast with its background, and at the same time a part of the design.

Posters Require Imagination

Poster design is especially challenging to an artist, because he must have an original idea in addition to using the full power of color and of design. It is true that we see countless photographic posters, all leaning heavily on the appeal to human interests and human weaknesses. Pretty girls, smiling babies, the happy grandmother, the person in pain or being ridiculed are constantly used to persuade us to buy things. This type of poster is so common and so lacking in good taste that its appeal is only momentary and superficial. Good poster artists do not use designs of this kind. They choose an imaginative, original idea and present it in the form of a symbol.

What Are Symbols?

When a child makes a drawing of a man, a few lines are enough to represent a figure. Circles for the head and the body, lines for the arms and the legs, a few lines or dots for the face, and everybody can quickly grasp the child's meaning. Yet his drawing is by no means complete. It has, however, the essential characteristics in their simplest form. This makes it a symbolic drawing.

In the same way, the poster artist must represent people, places, things, and even ideas, by his own symbols. Thus, three or four wavy lines symbolize the ocean; a rake or a hoe represents farm activities; a dove stands for peace.

When we reduce an idea to a symbol and also concern ourselves with the design of that symbol, we produce what we call *graphic design*.

Make a Poster

Think of something you might wish to persuade a friend to do, such as read, sew, travel, plant, or join a club. Can you think of a symbol for your idea? Travel, for example, might suggest a train, an airplane, a suitcase or a strip of tickets. Plant might recall brightly colored vegetables or fruit. Sew might suggest spools of thread or a pair of scissors.

As soon as you have a symbol — and it should be interesting and imaginative — your problem is to make a good graphic design of it. Are you traveling by airplane? You might reduce your symbol to a propeller, a wing, or an insigne of an airplane. Are you planting? Just a few carrots or radishes will be more effective than a large assortment of vegetables, or perhaps a rake, a straw hat, or a scarecrow come to your mind for that theme.

Now consider the colored papers that are at hand. Select a background

68. POSTER   *Jean Carlu*

This decorative treatment of a fish is an interesting example of how a realistic idea may be simplified and yet retain the essential characteristics of the subject. The brief, well-lettered announcement is a forceful part of the design.

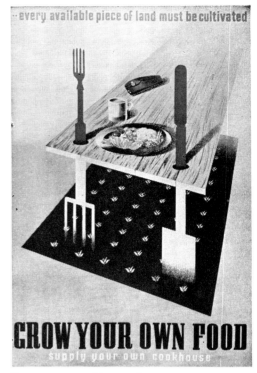

Matters of national importance are a challenge to the artist. He must teach the public a vital lesson while he makes an appeal that will have a lasting effect. This poster is unusually imaginative and persuasive.

69. POSTER   *Abram Games*

The power that a poster needs is strikingly illustrated here. We see a photograph which dramatizes a head and intensifies the texture of the skin; sun glasses symbolize the winter sport of skiing; sharp contrasts in tone — all combined to great advantage. The exaggerated difference in size between the man's face and the figure in the distant background is also effective.

70. POSTER   *Herbert Matter*

71. POSTER *E. McKnight Kauffer*

War posters are designed to arouse the emotions of people. This one achieves its purpose
by subtly suggesting both ancient and modern Greece. The head has a strong, sculptural
quality, and the light tones in the flag and in the lettering have been brilliantly planned.

73

This student made good use of her experience in cutting paper. By moving the separate parts of the design until they were placed in the most effective position, she arrived at a compact and well organized design.

This student cut out his design without any preliminary drawing. The forcefulness of the poster is due to its simplicity and to the good placing of the main shape and of the lettering.

72. POSTER *Student work*

73. POSTER *Student work*

color and test other colors with it. Plan color combinations you are sure will be effective from a distance. Odds and ends of scrap material are useful. Feathers, a fluff of cotton, corks, newspaper and corrugated paper, or string, can sometimes be used to form part of your design.

Select your colors and materials and, without any preliminary drawing, cut directly out of the paper the parts you need. Place them on the background, trying various arrangements and adding details necessary to make the whole design complete and effective. Now turn your attention to the lettering.

The Lettering Is Important

Since almost all posters carry a verbal message, plan a brief caption. A word or two may convey your meaning. The public likes to use its imagination, just as you do, and seldom pauses to read a long message.

The best type of lettering for posters is the capital block letter, that is, a heavy, bold letter of uniform thickness. Letters can be cut directly from paper without preliminary drawing. All the letters of the alphabet may be cut from a square except E, F, H, I, J, L, and T, which are narrower.

Choose a color for the lettering that is strong and will be effective when contrasted with other colors. Cut out the letters and experiment in placing and spacing them. Move and adjust all parts of the design until the lettering and the subject, combined, make a well-balanced unit. When you are satisfied with the result, carefully paste the pieces in position.

Criticize the Results

Exhibit your posters and those of your classmates. Discuss them and make suggestions for their improvement. If you have some professional posters available, consider them carefully to see if you think the artists were always successful in accomplishing their aims. Include posters on billboards, in buses, and in shop windows. Think of the messages they carry, and judge them also as examples of art. When you find some that you like, try to decide why you like them.

Practice What You Have Learned

You may help to improve poster design in your school by contributing to the many demands for posters throughout the school year, such as those for school elections, for parties, for clubs, for exhibitions, and for sports. Each type of problem should be a challenge to your imagination. You need not be able to draw a line, but with a good idea, you need only scissors, paste, and a collection of papers and other material to create a poster that will carry its message clearly and graphically.

Be critical of the manner in which posters are displayed in corridors, in elevators, or on bulletin boards. If posters are hung in a careless, helter-skelter fashion, swinging crookedly from one tack, they generally find their way very quickly to the waste-paper basket.

Other Types of Advertising

Other types of graphic design very similar in purpose to that of the poster but used in other ways and perhaps designed on a much smaller scale are needed also. Leaflets, book jackets, trademarks, pasters and stickers for baggage, for packages and for automobiles are all designed to call our attention in a brief, colorful way to an emblem, a name, a place, or a product.

You will find a wealth of free advertising material at hand for consideration, since all producers are more than anxious to distribute anything that will advertise their products. Folders, booklets, small posters, programs, bulletins, either stream through the mail directly to you or are set on counters or in the windows to attract your attention. Countless advertisements appear in magazines. Make a collection of the advertising matter you find interesting for some reason or other.

Study This Advertising Material

Bring your collection to class and contribute to an exhibition of advertisements by selecting and displaying a few of the things you like best. Now observe the entire collection carefully and you will see that the commercial artist uses color in a very purposeful way. Can you see how his mind works when he is trying to be most persuasive in advertising his product? Use the following check list to see if you can pick out, first of all, those advertisements which, in addition to being attractive, really advertise effectively.

1. Which is the first to attract your attention? Why?
2. Which holds your attention longest? Why?

76

A bold arrangement of intense colors has produced this vivid design. Graphic representation of every object in the illustration makes each one clear and attractive to the child.

Color and subject matter have been combined to give beauty to this label for a cigar box which serves both a practical and a decorative purpose.

74. ILLUSTRATION FOR CHILD'S BOOK *Leonard Weisgard*

75. TRADE MARK

3. Which arouses your curiosity? Why?
4. Which will you remember longest? Why?

Consider Color in Relation to Advertising

In your earlier studies you saw how effective color may be as a messenger to convey ideas and moods. Look carefully at the collection before you and see if you and your classmates agree on the answers to the following questions:

1. In which design is the color best used as the chief power in attracting attention?
2. In which is the color most effective from a distance?
3. In which design is the color used most imaginatively?
4. In which is the color best organized or distributed?
5. In which design does the color most effectively advertise the product? Do you find, for example, that pale, delicate colors are used for such things as perfume, dresses, handkerchiefs, or a book like " Baby's First Year "; that bright, gay colors are used for such things as kitchenware, outdoor furniture, and flower seeds; that exciting color is used for a theatrical event or for a fashion show?
6. Which advertisements would you choose:
   a. to place in a subway or bus?
   b. to send through the mail?
   c. to place on a bulletin board?
   d. to reproduce in a magazine?

Test Yourself in Advertising

At this point it will be interesting to see how well you can convey an idea, how quickly and effectively you can express it in such a way that everyone can at once understand and enjoy it. To prepare yourself for this task it would be well to try a few preliminary experiments.

Select a few colored papers to serve as backgrounds (use black and white also if you wish) and pin on each background a combination of two or more small pieces of colored paper. Hang them up at the front of the room and number them. Now observe carefully the power of the various color combinations to attract attention. Choose the best combination, the next best, and so on, and make a list, making the best one A, the second best B, and so on.

Work with your classmates, try to reach some general conclusions about which color combinations are strongest. Do your conclusions agree with these which are generally accepted by color experts?

1. Greatest visibility in color is achieved when there is a combination of three factors:
   a. Strong contrast in dark and light.
   b. Strong contrasts in intensity.
   c. Contrasts in warm and cool colors.
2. Certain contrasts in color (light against dark, bright against dull, warm against cool) are used over and over again because they are known to be effective. Some examples of such combinations are:
   a. Black on yellow.
   b. Yellow on black.
   c. Red on white.
   d. Yellow on blue.
   e. Orange on brown.
   f. Pink on black.

It is important to remember the color combinations that are strong and effective if you wish to work out any future problems in advertising or in displaying products.

Packaging Needs Color

Boxes and bottles, cardboard, glass, and plastic containers are no longer considered simply receptacles for the product within. When they are harmonious in color and in form, and the lettering is an integral part of the design, they attract the attention of the potential customer and add greatly to his impression of the value of the product.

Designers who work in the packaging field use color freely to attract the consumer. For example, we find on the labels of cigar boxes many rich, glowing colors which suggest a fragrant product from tropical climates. Brightly colored wrappings on cans of fruits and of vegetables are important in attracting the buying public. If we saw the bare tin stripped of its brightly attractive label, we could scarcely believe that within were delicious fruits or tempting vegetables.

78

This is also true in packaging chocolates and candy bars. Would they seem attractive if wrapped in, let us say, dull green paper? Shiny cellophane, gleaming bits of gold and silver, light, appetizing colors are unquestionably suggestive of the sweetness and the surprising delights to be found within the package.

Even medicines, cough drops, tooth powders, to mention but a few of the thousands of products we see daily, catch our attention by the bits of color that have been used to make them attractive.

If the problem of packaging interests you, there are many things that you can work out in this field. Choose a product which you constantly use and try to see if you can present it in a more attractive way than the one in which it now appears.

Display is the Thing

An object need not be costly in order to look attractive. Even the simplest gadget can be made to look impressive by the way in which it is displayed. We have come far since the time when all shop windows were stuffed full of every type of merchandise to be found within the shop. Today window dressing is considered an art. A few carefully selected articles are displayed in a setting that suggests where and how the article might be used. Bathing or summer-sports clothes, for example, are often placed in a setting of sand, shells, and palm trees, and the vivid play of color makes the clothes even more attractive and alluring. Quantities of kitchen utensils and kitchen hardware have little appeal, except to the most practical mind, but a few, dramatically arranged to reveal interesting contours and attractive materials, can easily attract the passer-by. Humor and imagination both play a large part in displaying commonplace things in a way that suggests that their daily use would be a pleasure to their owner. In every case it is the harmonious use of color, the fine balance and proportion of all parts of the display that make these arrangements as much a picture as a poster or a painting would be.

Arrange a Display

Would you like to try your hand at this new art? If so, take some small object that you have in your pocket or your handbag, such as a powder compact, a key, or perhaps a coin. Clear your desk and try to imagine it

76. MAGAZINE COVER *Student work*

The design for this cover was carefully organized. Its motif is a combination of two symbols: one for the school and another for an important event of that year.

77. BOOK PLATE *Student work*

The book plate, as well as any other form of label, may serve at the same time a decorative and a useful purpose. This one not only identifies the owner of the book but also describes the school buildings and how to reach them.

Kitchen utensils of fine design repeated in varying sizes emphasize the desirability of practical, useful kitchenware. The balanced, orderly arrangement of this display suggests a neat, modern kitchen.

A student used colored papers in her miniature display to create an appropriate setting for her little hats. The curled paper helps to unify the different parts of the design.

78. WINDOW DISPLAY

79. WINDOW DISPLAY *Student work*

as a small portion of a show case or a shop window. Plan a display of the object you have chosen considering ways to make it appear more important than it actually is. Do you think this could be done by:

1. placing it on a brilliant and contrasting color?
2. raising it from the desk level by means of a little platform?
3. placing it within a well-designed paper container?
4. placing it before an interestingly folded paper that is suggestive of a screen?

Select one of these methods, or one of your own devising, to display your object. Use cardboard, colored papers, or any other material and work with the one you choose until your result makes a compact design.

Look at all of the miniature displays that your classmates have made. Select the best and arrange them on a shelf as though they were being shown in a shop. In this arrangement be sure to consider that it is important to balance sizes and colors.

This first experiment naturally leads you to plan a more original and complete display for a particular product. For this, either bring some object or container from home or use one that you have designed. Consider how to exhibit it in an attractive way which brings out both its character and its qualities. For example, a bottle of perfume suggests something delicate, romantic, and expensive. The design on the jacket of a detective story suggests action and mystery, and these are associated in our minds with vivid, lightninglike contrasts. The title of the book itself should give you many interesting suggestions.

Try to associate interesting colors, contrasts in color, and exciting color combinations with the object you display. Texture can also suggest ideas, so your scrap pile of odds and ends will be useful.

Try Practical Window Designing

This venture into display will help you to appreciate the inventiveness and originality of good window dressers. Look about your own neighborhood. In how many shops is the merchandise well displayed? Could you make some practical suggestions for improvement to those who have neglected this art? If you have an opportunity to do a little work in actual window display in a store where you may be working, try to do so, thus putting the knowledge you have gained to good use. Be firm in your con-

Paper is an excellent medium for experiments in display. Students designed the flexible figures. The two lower designs illustrate the necessary relationship between a figure and its background.

80. WINDOW DISPLAY   *Student work*

81. WINDOW DISPLAY   *Student work*

viction that simplicity expresses refinement, good taste, and the inherent value of an object far better than gaudy showmanship can.

School Displays Need Assistance

Never lose an opportunity of applying your feeling for design to activities throughout the school. The range of school exhibitions is enormous and always stimulating, from seasonal displays at Christmas to the projects of individual departments. How much greater their appeal when color is used with good judgment! Well-lettered headings for exhibitions emphasize their message and add to its clarity. Carelessness and indifference in spacing and overcrowding of poorly selected material rob an exhibition of its effectiveness. Try to make art function successfully in the displays throughout your school.

Communities Need Help

Many a traveler to this country, surveying not only our city streets but also our country roads, has been shocked by the plague of advertising that has settled down, like the locusts, upon our land. Billboards, sides of buildings, barns, even roofs have been so thoroughly plastered with blatant and persistent advertisements that the beauty of our landscape is obscured beyond measure.

Make it your duty to employ good taste and discrimination in all matters of advertising. Be convinced yourself, then convince your community that business can be equally successful without overwhelming the people and the countryside with unrestrained advertising.

82. DIANA FASTENING HER CAPE *Greek, IV cent.* B.C.

Greek costume changed but little over long periods of time. Pieces of material cut according to a pattern were not used. Lengths of fabric were draped and pinned on the wearer, who adjusted the conventional styles to his or her own figure. Greek arrangement of drapery, with the beauty of its line and its fine use of the draping quality of the material, has frequently inspired the contemporary designer to attain a similar classical beauty in modern dress.

7.

COSTUME

ALL OF US like to masquerade, to change our appearance and our character. This desire to dress up is a natural form of self-expression for we believe that the appropriate costume can make us appear as important and impressive as we should like to be. How strong and manly a thin little boy becomes when he puts on football gear! The shy little girl, when in a drum major's costume, does not hesitate to strut along, leading her band.

Costume as a form of expression is as old as man's existence, and it has as many different forms as there are groups of people. The familiar term "putting on your war paint" comes to us from one of the many customs of the Indians. They quite naturally followed their instinctive desire to dramatize themselves with paint, masks, and costumes. In war and in peace, in religious affairs as well as those of home life, the dress of the Indian has always been important to him.

Throughout the world we find that the character, the customs, and the particular interests of tribes, of clans, and of nations have controlled not only their ceremonial costumes but also their everyday dress. Travelers have been fascinated by the rich and colorful variety of national costumes. A study reveals the rigid traditions that have controlled the styles and the colors for generations. We find not only distinctly national costumes but also clearly defined and strictly observed conventions which distinguish the costumes of regional groups within a nation or a country.

American Clothing

Though we have, as a nation, no national costume, as individuals we are considered very well dressed. Our costume at any time is controlled by the style of the period in which we live. We do not dress as our grandparents did, nor will our children dress as we do now. Our costume is an interesting and ever-varying combination of tradition and of new ideas, of fashion, and of good design.

The Old and the New

Our dress designers often base their styles on ideas obtained from traditional costumes. From costumes of the past they have learned the lesson of simplicity. We have only to look at Greek sculpture to be conscious of the simple and beautiful clothing that follows the form and the natural proportions of the human figure. Some other fashions, by contrast, are astonishing. Seventeenth-century costumes in France, because of their exaggerated disregard for the natural lines of the figure, could never be considered esthetically fine no matter how fashionable they were in their day. In line, in color, in fabric, and in form, our modern clothing does more than cover and protect the body; it enhances its natural beauty.

Dress designers are an inventive group. They take great liberties with traditional styles and use traditional materials in new ways. We find them choosing sports materials, such as cottons and woolens for evening wear, and the so-called dressy materials, such as satin and silk for bathing suits. Dress designers are always looking for new materials. Rayons, nylons, materials from plant fibers and synthetic substances are as common today as wool or cotton, linen or silk. And, in the work of the modern designer, there is an ever-increasing simplicity, less fussiness and overornamentation, more reliance on contrasts in color and in texture.

Fashion and Design

Costume design, more than any other art, is affected by changes of all kinds. New creations and variations of existing fashions appear constantly in all the clothing trades. This huge industry includes everything from the manufacture of buttons and thread to that of costly fur coats. Because of the rapidity of changes in the fashion world, our clothes, unless

83. COSTUME *French, XVII cent.*

84. COSTUME *French, XVII cent.*

In their own period these costumes were the height of fashion and an accepted part of the modes and manners of that day. Notwithstanding the fact that they were made with great skill from beautiful materials, we moderns cannot help but feel that though elegant, they are lacking in good taste. Accustomed as we are to simplicity, overornamented costumes, designed with little or no regard for the natural lines of the body, are something which we are happy to have left behind in the history of civilization. How would you like to wear one of these costumes now?

chosen with care, generally look out of date before they are worn out. Advertising, fashion shows, and the moving pictures contribute greatly to the public desire for new creations each season. Girls and women welcome change and wish each costume to be different from one already worn. Boys and men cling to one style for a much longer period and for that reason it is important that they consider their choices very carefully.

During school years we are inclined to be the slaves of fashion. We wish to wear only the styles current for our particular group and prefer to appear dressed, not as individuals, but as members of a group. We feel that we must wear the same kind of hat or cap, choose the identical shoes or jackets which our companions wear. It never occurs to us to question the beauty, the taste of these uniform trappings, nor yet to care whether or not they suit our particular style.

A little later we consider ourselves as individuals and think of clothes as a means of expressing our own individuality. We find pleasure in choosing clothes that suit our own personal taste and our own characteristic coloring.

We are naturally governed in our choice of clothes by our knowledge of color and of design. Let us consider how to add to our understanding of color and of design in costume generally and to the selection of clothing that is best suited to us, individually.

Select Colors with Discrimination

Colors affect us and we react, often unconsciously, to the colors of the clothes we wear. Some colors stimulate us, make us sparkling and gay; others depress us, or induce self-consciousness. The colors that make us happy are those we should choose to wear since, in most cases, they are the colors that are becoming to us.

Not only do we react individually to color in a costume but each one of us seems to have the power to intensify or to alter the quality of the colors we wear. Worn by one of us, a certain red, shall we say, is beautiful: on another it is ugly. The color itself seems to change with each wearer. A borrowed coat or dress may therefore appear entirely different when worn by someone other than its owner. Therefore, our choice of color for ourselves must be carefully considered. No matter how much we admire, let us say, a yellow sweater worn by a friend or by a popular actor or actress, we should not rush out to buy one for ourselves unless we really know

90

The originality of many primitive tribes is often shown by the way in which they used available materials for clothing which they designed to meet the necessities of their climate. They used the skin of animals for leather and for fur; they made cloth from the bark of the tree and from other natural fibers. These luxuriant Eskimo fur robes, with their interesting lines and beautiful embroideries, show a great feeling for design on the part of their primitive creators.

85. COSTUMES *Alaskan*

that it will be as becoming to us as it was to the person on whom we first saw it.

To know what colors suit us requires good judgment. In developing this judgment, we must try first to consider our own physical appearance: the color and the tone of the complexion, of the hair and of the eyes; the size and the proportions of the figure. Each of these factors should have a definite influence upon our choice of a color scheme. Certainly a blue-eyed boy or girl with a light complexion should not wear the warm and intense colors that are flattering to those who have brown eyes and a dark skin. Nor should one who is short and chubby select those assertive colors that require either height or slightness of build to be appropriate and becoming.

Before planning a wardrobe for yourself, you should know the effect of various colors on your individual coloring and personality. A study of various types of people will help you to recognize and to understand your own color type.

Experiment with Student Models

Look among your classmates for definite color types. These will include individuals with blond, brunette, black, light brown, or red hair; with ruddy, pale, sallow, tan, or fair complexion; with blue, brown, green, gray, or hazel eyes. Ask your models, both boys and girls, to stand at the front of the room. Hold various pieces of colored paper or fabrics under their chins. Study the effect of each color upon each model. Decide what colors you consider most becoming to each type. Test your choice by trying to answer such questions as:

1. Why are certain colors becoming to particular types of coloring? Is it due to contrasts between the color of the material and the coloring of the model? Are they:
   a. contrasts of hue?
   b. contrasts of light and dark?
   c. contrasts of bright and dull?
   d. contrasts of warm and cool?
2. Do the colors chosen help to accentuate the interesting aspects of the model's coloring? Do they emphasize the hair, or the eyes, or the complexion?

86. STAGE COSTUME   *Robert Edmond Jones*

Here an artist shows how he plans a costume design for the stage. After experimenting with materials to find color combinations and textural contrasts that pleased him, he designed the costume that would emphasize personality and be most effective and appropriate. Notice the play of light colors against dark and the use of yellow as a harmonizing color.

3. Is there a relation between the personality of the model and the intensity of the colors selected as becoming?
4. Do the colors selected add to the attractive appearance of the model?

It is as important to know why you reject colors as it is to know why you choose them. Did you reject certain colors for particular models for any of the following reasons?

1. The colors were too nearly like the natural coloring of the model.
2. The colors were too brilliant and attracted attention away from the individual.
3. The colors did not emphasize the most interesting coloring of the model.

Consider Your Own Type

Having studied others, you should now be able to analyze yourself and your own type of coloring. Examine yourself intently in a mirror, in all lights, until you are familiar with your own appearance. In the same way, study the effect on yourself of various colors to be found in your wardrobe. You may find that some are becoming to you, yet do not seem to express your personality, possibly because they are too pale, or too subdued, or too intense. Be sure to ask other students to help you in making final choices.

Experiments in Designing Costumes

The colors you have chosen for yourself will suggest particular types of costume to you. Choose one of the combinations and plan a costume for yourself, suited to a special use as for school, for sports wear, or for office wear. The colors chosen will determine to a great extent the color design of the costume. For example, a dark-green sports suit, revealing only a small amount of a light, yellow-green blouse or a tan shirt would create a very different color harmony from a costume in which the same colors were used in equal amounts, as in the combination of a yellow-green skirt with a dark-green sweater, or of tan slacks with a dark-green jacket. Colors may add to the effect of the height or the breadth of the figure; they may make the face more or less conspicuous. Study the changes that combined colors make in relation to your own figure.

Use colored paper, crayons, or paints to make at least three trial sketches with the color scheme you have chosen, each time changing the relative position and the proportion of the colors. If you use colored papers or fabrics, cut out the parts corresponding to the design of the costume you are planning and interchange the colors until you have three different arrangements. Mount all three on a sheet of paper. Study the different color combinations in relation to your own figure to see which seems to be the most flattering. In the proper position fill in a color for the face and for the hair to approximate your own coloring. You now have some suggestions that should serve as a guide in designing and in selecting costumes for yourself.

Patterned Materials Must Be Considered

Since many of the colors for our costumes include figured materials, woven or printed, such as plaids, checks, flower designs, and others that many like, we must consider both the color and the character of these designs. Do you not feel that a bold, striking pattern seems best suited to a person of vivid coloring and strong personality, while a delicate, small pattern suits a person whose coloring does not contain strong contrasts? Size and proportion of our figures should also be considered in selecting patterns for costumes, because our physical characteristics can be emphasized or subdued according to the material selected.

Patterns Create Variations

A costume, made in whole or in part of figured material, seems quite different from one made of a solid color. How well do you look in materials that are for example, striped, dotted, or flowered? Observe the other students; notice the various materials they are wearing. Every season brings forth new designs from which to choose; large or small, bold or subtle patterns, in bright or in subdued colors. Which type can you wear? With the help of a collection of odds and ends of materials that you may find at home and bring to class, you may study the effect of a variety of designs upon your coloring, your figure, and your personality. Are you the type that looks best in:

1. large patterns in vivid colors?
2. small patterns in either vivid or in subtle colors?
3. solid colors?

94

87. COSTUME FOR SECURI LAKITA DANCE   *Nilda Nuñoz del Prado*

This gay costume was worn in pre-Spanish days in Bolivia by the Aimaras Indian. Used in a dance of religious meaning, each part of it is traditional. Parts of it might easily be adapted to present-day wear. The accompanying textiles would be appropriate in color and in texture.

It will be clear, after a few experiments, that figured materials must be carefully chosen since they have a decided effect on our appearance. Indiscriminate or thoughtless selection can make one appear to be lacking in good taste and judgment. Here is a little questionnaire on the subject. Can you answer the following?

1. How do patterns affect a costume?
2. Is a large, bold design suitable only for something like a necktie, a scarf, or a blouse, or may it be used for an entire costume?
3. Are some designs more effective when used sparingly?
4. May all kinds of designs be used for the same style of costume?
5. Is a floral print appropriate for a tailored suit?
6. Do vertical or horizontal stripes appear to alter the proportions of a figure?
7. Is there any relation between the size and the type of the pattern and the size and the type of the person who can wear it?
8. Do several different types of figured materials combine well in one costume?

As you may realize, not all of these questions can be answered by yes or no. The subject is an intricate one and deserves your careful consideration.

Consider Texture of Fabrics

The color in a costume is definitely affected by the textural quality of the fabrics used. For this reason color cannot be considered apart from the fabric. Color quality and textural effects vary endlessly in the fabrics that are available today. We find rough, dull-surfaced materials that are in great contrast to those that are smooth or glossy. If we consider them carefully, we find that some weaves are firm and flat, while others are loose and coarse. By holding various fabrics up to one's face, one finds that some, because of the material and the weave, seem to absorb color, like linens and cottons, and so have a very different effect on one's appearance from fabrics that are smooth, silky, or glossy. We observe that strong features, high coloring, and sharp facial contours characteristic of some people may be heightened by fabrics which would overpower a person of delicate coloring or of a small, slight bony structure.

Experiments in combining colors and textures, in using wool, silk, cotton, feathers, yarn, and buttons, materials used by dress designers, led students to visualize new possibilities in creating costume ensembles.

88. COLOR AND TEXTURE   *Student work*

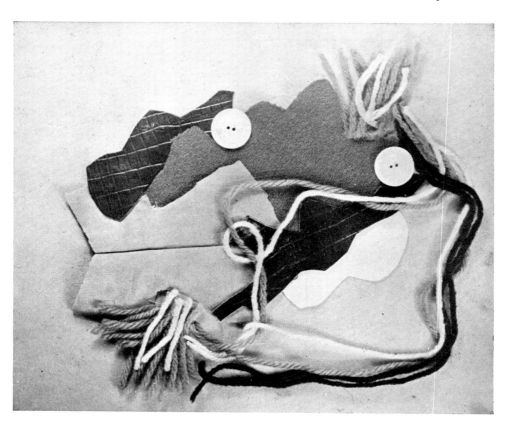

89. COLOR AND TEXTURE   *Student work*

Different Textures Vary the Costume

It is interesting to note the effect of textures on colors. We notice how different a certain red, for example, appears in velvet, in cotton, in a loose, woolly tweed, in a gleaming satin, or in a crisp taffeta. Also, we soon discover by experimenting with fabrics that the colors we have selected for ourselves are not always becoming in all types of fabrics.

With this fact in mind, choose a color that is becoming to you and is appropriate for a costume for fall or spring. Plan an ensemble, such as a coat and dress, or a suit and an overcoat, carefully considering the fabric to be used. Introduce textural variations to enliven the costume. Add any interesting contrasts in color you think advisable. These will add interest to the costume and must be carefully considered in order to maintain its unity.

Consider the Results

Arrange an exhibition of all the costumes planned by you and by your classmates and discuss them in relation to the persons for whom they were designed. Select those that are most successful and make suggestions for the improvement of those that seem less attractive.

The Old May Be Revived

Fabrics, in themselves, are interesting. Since clothing has always been one of man's basic needs, the art of making textiles has developed steadily from earliest times. In all parts of the globe fabrics have been produced from materials of the region that were appropriate to the climate and fulfilled the needs of the people. Into these handmade textiles have gone much of man's ingenuity and thought, not only in devising methods of weaving, in preparing and in dyeing wool, cotton, bark, and other fibers, but also in creating patterns and types of weaves. The textiles from the past are a great source of inspiration to us. Every season we may see a revival of interest in one or more of them, from primitive cotton prints to elaborate brocades.

Dressmakers Know Fabrics

We observe that various fabrics, because of their texture, have a character and suggest a style peculiar to themselves. Velvets, for example, seem dignified; they may be draped in long, classical folds. Chiffons are soft and graceful; they drape easily. Tweed suggests physical activity and creates a simple, clear silhouette. Taffetas and similar crisp materials are piquant and sharp in outline.

Professional designers, when creating a new costume, generally work directly with the material from which it is to be made. They study its texture; they experiment with it to see what kind of folds are produced when it is draped, twisted, or hung from a support. When they are satisfied with their study they drape the material on a figure to discover its most interesting possibilities. Then they create a costume which utilizes the draping qualities of the material, and a cutter makes a pattern from which the final model is to be made.

Try a Practical Experiment

Perhaps you sew or have watched tailors or dressmakers cut and make garments. While it requires skill to interpret dress patterns and directions accurately, this alone does not test your inventive powers nor your creative ability. Perhaps you might like to design a dress; to create something from your material that is appropriate to it. Boys should not forget that their clothes are designed for them by men, and that men have long been famous for their skill in designing for women as well. Why not experiment with some discarded piece of clothing? Consider how you can redesign and remodel it. You may wear or bring it to class as a proof of your ability to make a new costume out of an old one.

Unity Is Most Important

Interest in costume and a study of it leads us to realize that, if we wish to be well dressed, we must follow a plan which will include a whole wardrobe. Blouses, shirts, and coats must be considered in relation to the complete suit of which they are a part. Shoes, socks, hats, bags, gloves, and other accessories of costumes cannot be considered apart from the things with which they are to be worn. Many of us have received presents that were attractive in themselves, yet were not suitable for use with the rest of our clothing. Our wardrobe should be composed only of things that are a part of a unified design.

A student designed this thin metal lapel ornament, keeping in mind not only the shape of the ornament but also its relation to the background on which it was to be worn. The shiny metal makes an attractive spot against the rough woolen fabric.

90. ACCESSORY *Student work*

A spring ensemble, complete with hat, shoes, and bag, was designed by a student to suit her personality, her appearance, and her needs. She used actual bits of fabric to show the color and the texture of each garment.

91. SPRING ENSEMBLE *Student work*

Are You Well Groomed?

A person's choice of clothing and the way it is worn reveals character. Some people like to believe that baggy, loose, or careless attire expresses a happy, carefree nature. On the other hand, it is just as likely to make a person appear careless and irresponsible. The mirror, unfortunately, does not accurately reveal to us our own complete silhouette. We often concentrate on the face, the front of the hair, the lipstick or the tie, completely forgetting the part we do not see, the rear view. Well-cut and well-groomed hair, well-pressed and neat clothing are important factors in one's appearance and should never be neglected.

Summing up, it is an art to dress well. Good judgment in this art is developed through daily practice in planning what we are to wear each day. Selecting from your wardrobe the dress or the suit, and the blouse, shirt, shoes, and accessories to be worn with it, is as important as the purchase of a new costume. Those people succeed best at this art who can examine themselves without vanity; who can study themselves as they do any other design problem with which they are concerned.

8.

INTERIORS

WE SPEND A great part of our lives within doors. For many hours each day we are in our homes, shops, workrooms, or schoolrooms. Too often we accept our surroundings merely as places in which to live, to work, and to rest. The chief demand is that they meet our practical needs. Why should not all these places in which much time is spent be colorful and pleasing to our eyes? Seeing drab and uninteresting colors about us day after day, even though we are not acutely conscious of them, affects us unfavorably. Out-of-doors, nature supplies colors and tones in endless variety. Dark and light harmonies and changes in atmosphere subdue or heighten a never-ending variation of color from sunrise to sunset. Is it not possible to bring some of this color indoors for our own pleasure and satisfaction? Of course it is, but we must use color intelligently and harmoniously!

Color as a Soothing Influence

Home, office, factory, and schoolroom can provide relief and stimulus for bored or tired eyes. Even a small waiting room can extend a friendly welcome through its color. The nervousness most of us experience in new and strange surroundings, such as the waiting room of a doctor or a dentist, is minimized when fine, rich color is used instead of harsh whites, tans, or muddy greens. Modern psychologists have made good use of color in hospitals to brighten the spirits of the patients and make them forget their troubles.

The Spiritual Qualities of Color

We are aware of the fact that the impressiveness, dignity, and awe-inspiring qualities in the interior of beautiful cathedrals and other places of worship are heightened through color. Illumination, color, and texture, the brilliant glow of stained glass all play a great part in providing the warmth, richness, and emotional quality that is the essence of their spirit.

Color as an Aid to Business

A great deal of attention has been paid to planning unusual color schemes for business places. We find that owners and designers of hotels, restaurants, and moving-picture theaters realize the value of creating settings that will give their patrons the beauty that they may lack in their everyday surroundings. Color is constantly emphasized in commercial showrooms, in salesrooms, and in window displays. Long ago businessmen learned that color makes a substantial contribution to the success of an enterprise. Color impresses people as quickly and as effectively as an invisible, pleasant salesman.

Color as Part of Our Homes

To most of us home is one of the most important places in life. It should express, as far as we are able to make it, our personal taste and our own individuality. Who has not experienced delight and surprise upon unexpectedly entering a room that is beautifully arranged and unusually colorful? That same pleasure should be ours when we enter our homes.

Color in the home includes more than an occasional bright object, such as a vase or a sofa cushion. Every part of the house and everything in it plays a part in the color scheme. The walls, the floors, and the ceilings, the woodwork, the draperies, the rugs, and the numerous small things should all be related to one another in a well chosen plan.

Consider a Plan

We are naturally interested in applying our knowledge of color and of design to our homes. Let us be critical, for the moment, of the things we generally accept with very little question. Let us look about the room in which we are gathered. Which elements please us and which are those we should like to vary or to discard? Shall we start with the walls? They are in color. Are they satisfactory as they are or should they be lighter or darker, brighter or duller, warmer or cooler, rougher or smoother? Would you like to introduce other decorative treatments in which wallpaper or paints were used for additional color or texture?

Do you like the ceiling and the floor? Should they be in greater contrast with the walls or blend with them? Is the furniture harmonious or is it miscellaneous in character and lacking in color unity? Is the whole color arrangement haphazard or does it seem to be planned?

Our answers to these questions will naturally depend on our individual taste, our ideas of the function of a room, and the soundness of our feeling for color. The best way to clear up our ideas about interior design is to try some experiments that will help us to discover the important things about it. Are you ready to begin?

Experiment in Miniature

A good way to discover something about color in relation to walls, furniture, carpets, and drapery is to experiment with colors in a small model. For this experiment, take a piece of nine-by-twelve inch paper and fold over five inches of the length. This makes the corner of a room, with one long and one short wall. Next, at right angles to the first crease, fold over two inches of the paper. This makes a section of the floor. Fold down two inches of the remaining long edge and you have a ceiling. Cut through the two-inch creases on the floor and in the ceiling, overlap the ends, and pin them together. Now the little model will stand firmly enough to suggest a corner of a room. Take some colored chalks or crayons and you are ready to try different combinations of colors as decorative schemes for your room.

Choose and Combine Colors

Select one color for the floor, another for the ceiling, and either a third one for the walls or a different one for each wall. Apply the color lightly and evenly. When your room is finished, place it beside those of your classmates and study them all carefully. Do you see that:

1. Light and shadow appear to change the color of the walls, even though the same color has been used for both sides of the room? Do you find the same change in the walls of the room in which you are working?
2. The walls in shadow are darker than those receiving full light and their color seems less intense?

Because of these changes in the appearance of color, owing to light, some of us like to vary the color of the walls, making those that are in shadow lighter in tone than those that receive the light. With this color treatment, all walls will seem equally light. Another possibility is to make some walls brighter than others or to give some of them different colors. Are there examples of this type of wall coloring in the little exhibition before you? How do you like them?

Now study the collection of rooms to see if the color schemes seem to be appropriate for a particular type of room. Can you find those that suggest a living room, a bedroom, or a kitchen? Do you know why certain colors seem to belong in certain kinds of rooms? Do you like stimulating and unusual color combinations, or do you prefer those that are soothing and subtle? Is your choice due to your own personality or do you choose these combinations because you have definite reactions to colors in relation to various rooms and uses?

Add Furniture and Draperies

Make any changes you think necessary in your color scheme, then experiment with colors for furniture and draperies that might combine pleasantly with it. To do this, observe your long wall carefully. Visualize against the wall some piece or pieces of furniture, such as a large couch, or a desk and a chair, or a table and two chairs. You may include a window if you like. To represent the furniture you have chosen, cut separate pieces of paper or make little, three-dimensional models. Remember to keep them in scale with the room. A desk, for example, should be about one inch high to fit into your model.

The furniture you use in your little model may be thought of as being made entirely of wood, or it may be upholstered, or it may utilize a variety of materials, such as leather, rattan, or a handwoven fabric. Fabrics may be in solid colors or have figured, plaid, or striped designs. Color the furniture in tones you think would look well with your color scheme. Study the placing of each piece carefully, then pin or paste it in place.

Study the Class Results

1. In which rooms would you prefer to live?
2. Do you prefer those that are strongly contrasted in color or those that are closely related in color?
3. Do you like the rooms in which the furniture is emphasized through contrast in color with the walls or floor, or do you prefer furniture that is similar in tone to the background?
4. How many types of figured materials can be combined successfully in one room? If the rug has a design, would you use patterns on the couch and on the draperies?
5. Does it seem to you that the use of allover patterns for walls, rugs, draperies, or accessories depends upon the size of the room in which they are to be used?

The little models you made are simply trials from which a more detailed color scheme may be planned. Before working out a more elaborate model, let us pause to consider an important factor in all interior design; namely, the use of texture.

Introducing Texture Again

You have had some experience in understanding the part texture plays in affecting the quality of color. Now you can see how your knowledge can be of practical value. Let us begin one of the most fascinating of studies: the collection of samples of fabrics, floor coverings, wood veneers, wall papers, and other materials used in decoration. In every possible source look for materials that are interesting either for their glistening surface, such as polished wood, glazed chintzes, upholstery satins, or for the rich luster found in such materials as velvets and thick rugs, or for variety of weave found in many handwoven fabrics. Notice that some materials have a rough and sturdy character while others seem delicate and fragile.

With a collection of samples at hand you may study the effects of such things as a rough fabric against a smooth wood surface; a transparent fabric against a window; a shiny fabric against a dull one. Since too great a variety of textures is not desirable in room decoration, it is important to learn to select only those contrasts that will enrich and emphasize the color scheme.

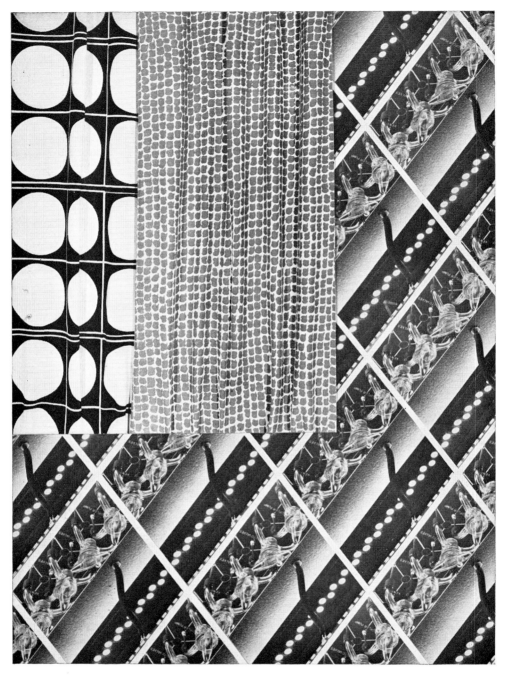

92. PATTERNS

In the upper left-hand corner we find two textiles, designed for drapery or for furniture. Both designs show a repeat of a single shape, but one is delicate and inconspicuous, the other bold and striking. In what kind of a room and with what other things do you think each would look best? The third pattern is made by repeating a photograph taken through a microscope. When designing fabrics, textile artists find inspiration in unusual subjects such as this.

93. FABRICS *Dorothy Liebes*

Texture, as well as pattern, plays an important part in interior design. Woven textiles, such as these which have been designed for the machine by a contemporary designer, suggest modern furniture and modern interiors. Present-day taste approves the use of woolen, of cotton, and of rayon fabrics, rather than those of silk or of brocade.

Fabrics Must Be Appropriate

Certain fabrics, such as velvets, brocades, satins, laces, and embroideries, suggest or recall a period of long ago and a way of living far different from that of today. We realize that these materials belong to types of rooms and furnishings of bygone days. For example, heavy, elaborately woven tapestries are suitable only for a large, formal room. The furniture must be correspondingly heavy. Satins and brocades call for elaborate and delicate furniture. If we use such rich materials today, present-day standards of taste dictate simplicity of treatment. Loops, bows, ruffles, complicated methods of upholstering and of draping seem to us moderns like too much frosting on a cake. More and more we are relying on modern fabrics made especially for our present-day needs. Simple lines, interesting contrasts in color and in texture have taken the place of luxurious fabrics.

Furniture and Fabrics

Too often, furniture in a home is part of an odd collection, acquired at different times and with little relation to the room it now occupies. For many people, unfortunately, the possession of a number of comfortable and practical pieces of furniture, whether they relate to the design of the room or not, is completely satisfying. Grandma refuses to part with a single piece of furniture that she had when first married. Dad has his favorite chair, mother hers, and so it goes.

If anyone with a sharp eye glances over the fabrics to be found in many of our homes, he discovers in them this same conglomeration. Velours, brocades, damasks, and taffetas, in floral, striped, and miscellaneous patterns may be found in the same room. Do you think that all these fabrics and patterns should be put together? What would a well-trained decorator think?

Some Basic Ideas about Interior Design

If we agree upon some general ideas on home decoration, we shall find it easier to select or to create harmonious color schemes for our rooms. Do you believe in the following statements?

1. A room should be comfortable, to meet the needs of the family.
2. A room should be considered as one unit in line, in tone, and in color. Its elements should be unified.
3. Furniture should be selected both for suitability and for its part in completing a harmonious design.
4. Fabrics should be appropriate to the type of room in which they are to be used. The use of too many different types of patterns and textures should be avoided.

New Designs for Living

How would you improve a room in your own home? You are now well prepared to do this because you have had experience with color and texture, and you have learned to consider the qualities and the proportion of color in relation to various uses. Here is an opportunity to put your knowledge to practical use.

Study the particular room you have decided to improve. Ask yourself these questions:

1. Is the furniture adequate for the family's needs and is it well placed for comfort?
2. Is the room overcrowded with furniture and bric-a-brac; is it too sparingly furnished?
3. Is the whole color effect pleasant or do certain features disturb you?
4. Has the room an especially attractive feature, such as an unusually high ceiling, a very broad window, or a fireplace, and is that feature properly emphasized?

Let's Get to Work

Two walls and a floor are sufficient to make a three-dimensional model unless you prefer to include all four walls. You may cut down a cardboard box or make one of paper that is in proportion to the room you are to improve. Half an inch to a foot is a good scale. You now have the barest essentials with which to start your problems in interior design. Select the furniture you plan to keep. To represent these pieces, you may cut out paper shapes or construct small, three-dimensional models. Remember that the furniture should be kept in scale with the little room.

Now consider the color problem. Are you planning to use the present color scheme or parts of it because you like it, because you consider it appropriate, or because the family likes it? If not, hunt through your early color experiments to see if you have another color scheme you might prefer. Or you may select some scraps of colored paper that seem to be the basis for a good color scheme for a room. Consider the color of the floors, the walls, and the ceiling. Put these colors aside for a moment and think about the furniture. Here again, you are faced with the problem of combining colors. Does the main piece of furniture, the couch or the piano, for example, provide an interesting color note, one that contrasts with the general color scheme or is in close harmony with it? If it does, keep that color note, then select other colors that you think might go well with it. If you are dissatisfied with the color that is already there, select a new one and others that might harmonize with it.

After thoughtful planning you are ready to color your model room. Using chalks, paints, crayons, or colored paper, apply the colors to the floor and walls. As you do this, consider them carefully, studying the little room both in sunlight and by artificial light. Make any desirable adjustments in your first color plan, then turn your attention to the furniture.

Consider Color, Texture, and Pattern

Color your little models of furniture, starting with the most important piece, then the smaller ones. When using color, remember that you may suggest texture by the way you apply the color. The material that you suggest may be rough or smooth; it may be one color or several to suggest a weave or a print; it may have a pronounced allover pattern of some sort. Apply the color lightly at first so that you may change it if desired.

Arrange for Comfort and Harmony

Place your furniture in the model room, moving it about, playing with it, trying out all sorts of ideas and arrangements until you find one that pleases you. Ask yourself these questions about it:

1. Will the arrangement meet the needs of the family? Is it sociable; are the tables and lamps conveniently placed?
2. Does it seem relaxed, informal, and inviting?

94. COLOR, TEXTURE, AND PATTERN   *Handwoven textiles, Dorothy Liebes*

With bits of material such as we find here, you might plan the decoration of an entire room. Can you find here surfaces which you think might be pleasant in woodwork, in carpets, in drapery, and in furniture? Would you choose light colors, dark colors, or those that are contrasted in light and dark? Do you prefer warm colors or cool colors, or a certain quantity of each? Obviously, not all of these colors and textures would be used in one room.

3. Has the room a main point of interest?
4. Has it a definite color appeal? Is it soothing or stimulating; subtle or challenging?
5. Are the contrasts in color balanced and repeated throughout the room?
6. Are the textures interesting and varied; the patterns not overdone?

Make necessary changes in the color scheme of your model room. Add furniture, lamps, or ornaments that are needed. Next consider the treatment of the windows.

The Window Is Part of the Design

Windows are an important part of the design of a room. Each window serves more than a practical purpose, for there are many ways of using draperies, curtains, and blinds that are ornamental as well as useful.

Consider a window in terms of design. Do you wish to stress height or width in your room? Do you want the window to be conspicuous as a decorative feature or must it be an inconspicuous part of the wall? Consider how you can use lines and colors to accomplish your purpose, then add the blinds and drapery. For this purpose colored paper is excellent as you can easily cut or fold it for side draperies in curved or in straight lines and make a valance, or a band to run along the top of the window as, for example, a horizontal strip with straight, curved, or irregular edges. Venetian blinds may be suggested by neatly folded paper. Surface designs may be added to plain paper or real fabrics may be used. But regardless of the material used, the color, the patterns, the texture, and the line directions are the most important considerations.

Were You Successful?

Examine the designs of your classmates. Ask questions about them. Consider the problems they had to meet in redesigning their rooms and decide whether you would have solved them in the same manner.

Now make a little test. Take your design home and show it to the family. You may be acclaimed or you may be adversely criticized, but as your effort must meet with family approval, you will without doubt be interested in knowing how many people you have pleased and how many needs you have successfully met.

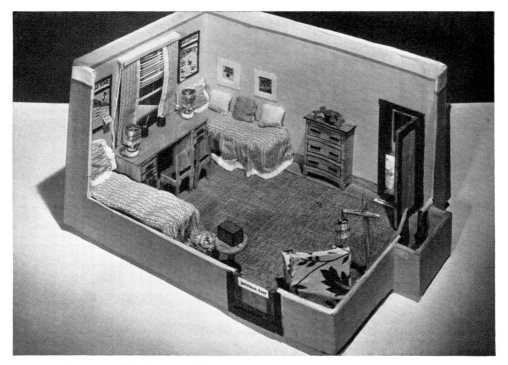

95. GIRLS' ROOM *Student work*

This study-bedroom for two girls was designed by a student. In addition to making both a comfortable and a pleasing arrangement of the furniture, she planned for adequate storage space and good reading light. A dressing table is placed in a recess behind the open door.

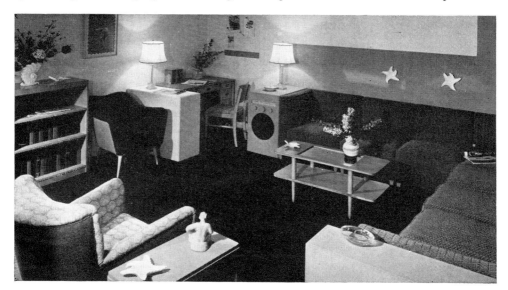

96. LIVING ROOM *Student work*

A student planned this room, which is informal and modern. She used deep, rich blues, contrasted with small, brilliant spots of contrasting colors. Low furniture and an emphasis on the horizontal line rather than on the vertical give her room the stamp of the modern designer.

New Fields for Interior Design

Have you not found it challenging to your ingenuity to plan and redecorate a room? Although it is seldom possible for us to discard what we have and to start with everything new, it is fun to try to design a completely new home or a room for ourselves.

Would you not like to design for yourself the perfect room, the room of your dreams? You can imagine living in a country cottage, a city mansion, a penthouse, an artist's studio, or even a trailer. You may have a swimming pool or a game room; a terraced sunroom or a cleverly compact kitchenette. At last you may have a room that is a complete expression of your personality; one that is perfect in proportion, in color, and in arrangement. You have but to make your choice and it is yours.

The Perfect Room

Make a list of the principal objects the room will contain. Must the room be especially planned to accommodate them? Think this over carefully, then consider the floor plan. Is it to be oblong, square, L-shaped, or perhaps oval? Consider the windows and the doors, making little sketches of each wall to help you plan them. You are now working with a vital part of the design, for these openings not only give access and light to the room but also greatly affect the remaining wall space. Wall spaces and windows make a pattern within the room as well as on the outside of the building. For this reason, architects think as much about the design of the interior as of the exterior. The resulting spaces, if well planned, will be exactly the right size and shape against which to set or build furniture.

With a plan in mind for a well-proportioned room, you are ready to create it. Construct or represent it as you wish, using cardboard or paper, or simply show it as a flat floor plan. Develop it in color, using a variety of media: paints, chalks, paper, or fabrics.

When your model shows fine proportions, with interesting windows and doors, draw any built-in features on the flat plan or construct them in three dimensions. These features would include not only closets but also built-in units of furniture, such as radio, bookcases, shower bath, and other structural parts of the room. Add the furniture after spending some time in planning its arrangement. Form interesting groups, formal or informal, as conversation groups and also plan to take care of individual interests and needs.

Now comes the pleasure of applying colors and fabrics to walls, floor, ceiling, furniture, and decorative items. Your color scheme may be as dramatic, as conservative, as original as you wish, if only it expresses your own personality. Consider carefully every step. Plan especially for a good distribution and balance of color, not only in relation to an individual area, but also to the harmony of the room as a whole.

Evaluate the Results

Invite a group of outsiders to act as jury for this problem. Perhaps an advanced art class might be happy to serve. Suggest that the rooms be judged by choosing the one that

1. is the most original in idea;
2. is the most inviting;
3. is the most stimulating;
4. is the most practicable;
5. is the most restful;
6. shows the best distribution of color;
7. has the best arrangement of furniture;
8. excels in craftsmanship.

Continue Your Experiments

All these experiments have no doubt shown you the nature of interior design. Your acquaintance with fabrics and furniture, your ideas about designing rooms will develop as you examine pictures in magazines or observe store displays with a keener eye. Watch for exhibitions, in museums and stores, of new designs in furniture, of new materials and their new uses. Choose the things that you like best in order to test your judgment.

When the opportunity comes to buy fabrics or furniture, or to plan redecoration of your home, try first to make a plan of your whole scheme. Study all varieties of colors and all kinds of materials. Make trial sketches or models as you did in previous exercises.

Practice designing by attempting rearrangements at home or in class.

97. LIVING ROOM   *Eugene Schoen & Sons*

Each room of a home should be esthetically enjoyable as well as practical. Here we find walls which are attractive for the quality of their unpainted wood. A boldly patterned drapery contrasts effectively and pleasingly with a plain carpet.

98. SALESROOM   *Eleanor Le Maire and Charles W. Beeston*

The designers of this salesroom achieved a desired feeling of space and airiness by a skilful arrangement of massive pieces of furniture.

Move furniture about; repaint it; pin up drapery at a window; arrange a plant, a vase of flowers, books or other objects to form interesting groups that contribute to their surroundings. Improve through practice so that your taste and judgment may give your own home an individual and inviting atmosphere.

Facts about House Paints

For those who like to do painting jobs about the house, we offer a little practical advice about the various kinds of paint.

Three kinds of paint are commonly used. First, the flat paint, which is made of powdered colors mixed with linseed oil. This paint can be thinned out with linseed oil and turpentine if too thick. Flat paint is generally used for walls because it gives a dull finish rather than one which is shiny.

Lacquers and enamels are made with powdered colors, but they have a varnish base. Neither linseed oil nor any other kind must ever be added to them, although they may be thinned out with turpentine or varnish. On surfaces that must be cleaned often it is best to use enamel paint which has a glossy finish.

Finally, there are water-base paints containing a variety of substances such as plastics or caseins to give them the proper consistency. These may be thinned out only with water. They give a dull, or mat finish. Since water base paints are easy to mix and to apply, they are used a great deal in the decoration of rooms, even though they are less durable than flat paint or enamel.

You May Mix Your Own Colors

It is possible to mix every imaginable shade with each of these three types of paint. However, only similar types may be used in mixing new shades. To the flat oil paint, one may add similar oil paints or even artists' oil paint from tubes if one desires a particularly interesting tone that may be achieved only by the addition of a small amount of a strong or fine quality of color.

To the water-base paints one may add poster, tempera, or dry-powder paints mixed with water.

To vary the color of enamel paints, only powdered paints mixed with a varnish base may be added.

In mixing paints it must be remembered that color samples made up in one type of paint can never exactly match another type. Therefore it is necessary to mix and to experiment with color in the paints to be used. In planning colors for walls, good-sized samples should be pinned on the walls in various parts of the room and the effect of light on the colors should be carefully studied. However, remember that color, when spread over an entire wall, will seem brighter than when seen in a small amount.

This drawing was inscribed on one of the walls of ancient Pompeii. Its spirit is conveyed by the upright carriage of the figure bearing a palm, a symbol of victory. Brief and forceful in character, it acquaints us with these people of long ago.

The names of some North American Indians, such as Curly Bear, Lazy Boy, Wades-in-Water, and Berry Woman are represented by these picture words, or pictographs. How many can you identify? For thousands of years not only names but also ideas have been communicated through this simple form of graphic art.

CAMPANI VICTORIAVNA
CVMNVCERINIS PERISTIS

99. GRAFFITO *Pompeiian*

100. SYMBOLS *American Indian*

9.

GRAPHIC ARTS

WHEN WRITING LETTERS to the family or to a good friend, have you not often wanted to add a few sketches to make your descriptions clearer and livelier? We find it delightful to receive a letter which illustrates the things described. These sketches we call graphic drawings for although the word graphic refers primarily to the art of writing, it is today also used to describe vivid, meaningful drawings.

Relation between Writing and Drawing

Drawing and writing developed together; both are ways of communicating ideas. The earliest methods of recording facts and ideas were to draw or cut lines on a clay or stone surface. These simple line pictures finally became the alphabet of a complete picture language. The hieroglyphics of the ancient Egyptians and the Mayans are examples of this picture language. Through the use of this graphic picture writing entire stories were cut into stone surfaces. These stories can still be seen engraved on ancient buildings and monuments.

The Development of Our Alphabet

As time went on, the picture language was found cumbersome and impractical. Gradually the art of writing was developed. Lines were used to make symbols which represented sounds rather than pictures or ideas. Thus, modern alphabets gradually developed. By means of it we write the spoken word. Each individual letter, A, B, C, and so on, is a symbol so designed that it is compact, simple to recognize and to remember. Each letter has a special shape and structure. The development from complex picture writing to the use of letters is parallel to all types of expression in art. To be brief, clear, and to the point was as necessary to the art of writing as it is to any form of art, particularly graphic art.

We All Drew

When we were very young, we loved to make pictures of familiar things. It was simple to draw the sun and the moon, a house, a plane, a flower or a tree. Almost unconsciously we selected the characteristic lines and shapes of things, creating symbols that represented the essentials of the subject. A circle for the sun; a crescent for the moon; oblongs, squares, circles, and a few wavy lines for smoke made a train. We did not draw from the actual object but from our memory of its main characteristics. This was for us the first step in graphic drawing. We found that we could tell stories simply through drawing. The difference between an apple tree and a Christmas tree, for example, was easily explained without the use of lengthy descriptions. In the same simple manner we were able to draw our houses, or Easter rabbits. How many of us can still do as much?

Drawing Is an Adventure

Let us try again to recover the instinctive impulse to draw which we once possessed. Let us try to be as unafraid and direct as in those early times before we learned to write or spell. To this natural way of working we must add the power of observation which includes a sharp, penetrating, keen analysis of the essential characteristics of the things, the people, and the places that we observe.

Keep a Daily Sketchbook

Sketching requires neither great preparation nor complicated materials. Paper or a sketchbook that you make for yourself out of inexpensive paper, a fairly soft pencil, a fountain pen or a medium-sized lettering pen and india ink are all that you need. Carry these articles with you and take the time to jot down quick sketches of what you see. The lines of these drawings may be very simple, but you must try to make them as

120

101. SKETCHES *Hans Albers*

These sketches illustrate a letter describing a trip to a strange town. The writer added them to his letter to make it more vivid and entertaining. The drawing below was made by the same person. This time he described things like trees, roads, and fences with vigorous, dark lines and with strong, black areas. The clear, sparkling quality obtained by contrasts in black and white makes this a good example of graphic design.

102. SKETCH *Hans Albers*

121

descriptive of the subject as possible. You will find it fascinating to exercise your powers of observation, to select and to remember the important lines of something you have seen, possibly for just a moment or so. Your subject may be anything that strikes your eye; a mop and pail, a man in the subway train, a woman in a market, a park scene, a flower, or a tree. Whatever you choose to draw, concentrate on setting down only its most characteristic and revealing lines.

Try Drawing from Memory

Try to memorize the lines that seem to be most expressive of various familiar subjects. Examine your surroundings as you go to your daily work with the eye of the artist who sees and memorizes everything of interest. Think of the upright line of a telephone pole beside a curving road, the angles made by the awning over the corner fruit stand, as characteristic lines that describe in unmistakable fashion some of the familiar scenes of everyday life. Try to see how well you can recall the interesting things you have seen by sketching them for others to enjoy.

Moving Lines Are Exciting

For sketching practice you will find it interesting to try gay and lively scenes. A few lines in a sketchbook may record a speeding train, a swing moving to and fro, a whirling merry-go-round, a trapeze artist high above the ground. Amid the movement and the excitement of such scenes you will find it difficult to jot down more than the most striking lines of some part of the action or scene. These notes, however, should serve later as a basis to which details may be added from memory.

Imagination Is Important

For the present it is not necessary to know scientific rules of drawing. It is far better to learn to rely upon your own observation. Train your eye to compare the size and position of objects in relation to one another. If you observe the direction of lines and of planes carefully, and if you study the effects that distance creates in the size and shape of objects, you will grasp the fundamental meaning of drawing by means of your own observation. Your imagination is important in helping you to catch the

With a steady, even contour line a young student has made an excellent caricature of himself, a tall, lanky schoolboy. The exaggerated length of the body, the amusing features, and the simplicity with which it was drawn intensify the humor of his drawing. Could you do as well?

103. CARICATURE *Student work*

The drawing below of an Indian woman grinding corn is not a caricature but a free interpretation of a subject. We notice that the artist, whose work you also saw in illustration 32, has exaggerated the curved lines of the figures as well as those made by the forceful direction of the arms. The simple, rhythmic line emphasizes the movement of the figure.

104. INDIAN WOMAN GRINDING CORN *Jean Charlot* *123*

spirit of what you have seen. Two or three suggestive lines may impart this spirit to your drawings. Make a number of drawings in various media and based on various themes, analyzing them for expressive and dramatic quality.

Elements of Graphic Drawing

All types of lines and countless variations in the use of black, white, and intermediate tones are the means by which a graphic artist expresses himself. With pen points of different widths and india ink try all possible varieties of lines, tones, and textures. Lines may be curved, straight, or zigzag. They may also be short strokes or long, unbroken, smoothly flowing contours. At times short lines or dots are repeated over an area to express something of the texture of the object and to show tones varying in light and dark, or they are introduced to aid in the representation of depth and solidity. A heavy, wide line may accent important parts of a drawing. Light lines may suggest the sensitive, delicate qualities of a subject. Parts of a drawing may be filled in with solid black to set off by contrast the more important parts of a composition.

The Art of Block Printing

If you recall attempts to use a toy printing set, you will remember how entertaining the experience was. You inked the surface of a block or stamp on which a letter had been raised and, by pressing it on paper, obtained a print.

Today we see only occasional bits of hand printing, since almost all printing is done by machine. It is difficult to realize that until medieval times lettering was done by hand and by only a few skilled artisans. Few people then could read or write. It was the invention of the printing press, with its use of movable letter types, that gradually put books into the hands of people. It was also found possible to print illustrations, either separately or simultaneously with blocks of letters, by cutting or engraving them on similar blocks of wood. All of such prints made from wood blocks are called woodcuts or wood engravings. Other materials, such as linoleum blocks and rubber plates are used today in a similar fashion for block printing all kinds of designs. This process of printing is called *relief* printing.

Jonas miffus eſt in mare·ꝛ ꞇeglutiꞇ a piſce·Jone
pꝛimo ca.   Jonas ꝟer ꝓphet warꝺ gewoꝛffen in ꝺaſ
mõꝛ vnꝺ von ꝺem walfiſch verſchlicket.

Scꝺa figuꞇa·
¶Sepultuꞇam ꝓi etiam filij Jacob ꝓfiguꞇaverũt.
Qui fratrem ſuum Joſeph in cyſternam miſerunt·
Filij iacob fratrem ſuum ſine cauſa vſꝗ aꝺ moꝛtem
oꝺerunt·Jta iuꝺei fratrem ſuum ꝓm gratis oꝺio ba
habuerunt·Filij iacob fratrem ſuum ꝓ triginta ꝺe=
narijs venꝺebant.Juꝺei ꝓum pꝛo triginta ꝺenarijs
iuꝺa emebant.Filij iacob tunicam fratris ſui ꝺilace
rauerũt.Juꝺei carnem ꝓi virgis flagellis ſpinis cla
uis verberauerunt·Tunica ioſeph nõ ſenſit aliquam
penam vel ꝺoloꝛem. Seꝺ caro ꝓi in omnibꝝ mẽbꝛis
ſuſtinuit paſſionem.Tunica ioſeph vſꝗ aꝺ talos ꝺe=
ſcenꝺebat. Et in ꝓo a vertiꞇe vſꝗ aꝺ talos nulla ſa/
nitas erat.Filij iacob tunicã ioſeph ſanguiẽeꝺi aſp=
gebant.Seꝺ iuꝺei tunicam Criſti ꝓꝛopꝛio ſanguine
pfunꝺebant. Filij Jacob patrem ſuum nimis turba
uerunt.Sic iuꝺei marie triſticiam maximũ intulerꞇ
Joſeph fratribus ſuis ꝗ in eo ꝺeliquerant relaxauit·

---

105. MEDIEVAL MANUSCRIPT   *German, XV cent.*

This page is an example of the decorative quality and of the beauty of hand-lettered
pages combined with a woodcut. The monks of medieval days lettered manuscripts
by hand, since printing from movable type had not yet been invented.

Here a group of gossiping women is the center of interest. The detail of the figures and the areas surrounding them are in decided contrast to the large, unbroken black and white spaces. Linoleum tools were used to cut out the white lines and spaces.

This student made a pencil drawing of his sister, then transferred the drawing to a piece of linoleum and cut it out. The continuous, steady line shows the descriptive power of a well observed contour. A white line on a black background such as this is often more effective than one made by pencil on white paper.

106. LOCAL EVENTS CLUB *Student work*

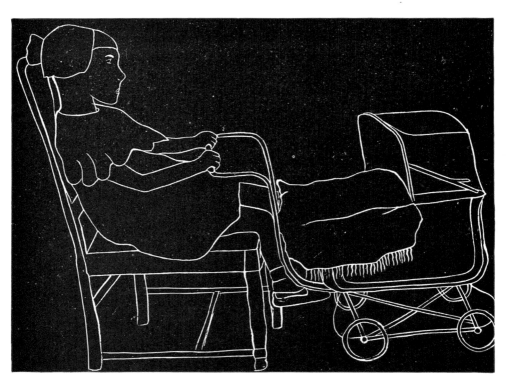

107. MY SISTER *Student work*

First Experiments in Block Printing

You can try many experiments of your own by using materials you have on hand and simple tools. A surface that can stand some pressure will give you an opportunity to study the principle of block or relief printing. For example, take a common soap eraser, a cork, or half a potato. Draw a simple design on the flat surface of one of them. Cut away the background with a knife. Thus the design remains above the background. This is the surface that is inked or painted with water color. Then it may be printed on paper.

Experiment with your block. Cover a fairly large piece of paper or cloth with some form of repeated design or allover pattern. For this purpose a rubber stamp pad or a pad of cotton covered with cloth may be used for inking the blocks you have cut. Saturate the pad with ink, dye, or tempera paint. Try to ink and to print your block evenly.

Cut a large number of different designs and print them, alternating small and large units. Plan different designs by repeating them and experiment with interesting color harmonies.

Decorative Printing

These trial papers printed with allover patterns may be sufficiently decorative to use as book covers, as gift-wrapping papers, or for construction work. With the same process you might add blocks that have letters or words cut into them. You will see the harmony between printed letters and printed patterns and realize how well they may be related in a design.

Further Experiments

After practice in this simple method of cutting a block and printing from it, you may be eager to try more difficult designs. Perhaps you would like to reproduce one of the drawings or compositions in your sketchbook. For this purpose select a drawing composed of a few simple lines and shapes. Trace the drawing on the surface of a linoleum block which should be a little larger than the drawing. For cutting you will need a knife or, better yet, a set of linoleum cutting tools. Care must be taken in using the cutting instruments. Your left hand must always be kept back of the tool so that, if it should slip, you will not cut yourself.

The lines of your drawing should be cut out of the surface of your block. In addition, you may cut out some other parts where you think some light areas will add to the effectiveness of your design. These areas may be cut out completely or some small, irregular surfaces may be retained.

Printing the Block

When you have completed the cutting, ink the surface of the block with printing ink, applying it thinly and evenly with a rubber roller. A primitive but effective method of printing is to place the paper, slightly damp, if possible, on the inked block and then to rub the back of the paper firmly and evenly with the back of a spoon or the handle of a knife until all the ink on the block is transferred to the paper. This process is known as making a rubbing and it was used in the very early history of relief printing. If you have a printing press, you can produce prints much more quickly than you could by the rubbing method.

Study your print carefully to determine if further cutting will improve it. Clean the block, work over it, and reprint until you are satisfied with the results. By keeping a print of each stage you will have an interesting record of your experiments.

Attempt More Ambitious Themes

Select another drawing from your sketchbook. Change it if necessary, to improve the composition. Add details needed to complete the theme or to make it more interesting. Trace the composition on a linoleum block. Before you begin to cut the block, review your previous experiences in block cutting. Remember that the uncut surface of the block produces a black area when printed. Therefore, retain large areas of black and cut away only those sections that you wish to show in strong contrast to the black. Remember also that the areas you cut out may be either a clear white or an intermediate tone, or value of black and white, according to your treatment of them.

In cutting do not try to incise lines or cut out areas that exactly follow your drawing. Work freely and use your cutting instrument to create suggestions of value and texture. The free and experimental use of your tools will, if well done, result in a print that has the characteristic style of the block print.

108. COUNTRY STORE *W. E. Phillips*

In this block print, variety in cutting enriched the black and white areas. The artist shows how the gouge may suggest textures of grass, of foliage, and of buildings. The clarity of the print is due to clean and deep cutting of lines and of areas, and to careful printing.

109. STEEPLECHASE *Louis Breslow*

Here is a block print that tells a story graphically by sharply silhouetting horses and riders against a clean white background. Exaggeration of movement and of expression also helps to depict a spirited scene.

Examine Your Results

There will always be surprises when you have pulled a print. If the block was evenly inked and enough pressure used in printing it, an even, clear impression should result. The print should be much more striking than your drawing, even though it lacks details. Brilliant black and strong white areas, together with intermediate tones suggestive of colors and of textures will add to the vividness of the original drawing. By now you must realize that the subject of your design is less important than its black and white arrangement. If you are not satisfied with your print, you may use the same drawing again, first rearranging the black and white areas. You may find that you should keep more areas black and reserve the white spaces for the most important parts of the composition. It is possible, if you wish, to reverse the dark and light scheme by cutting away the background and allowing the lines of your original drawing to remain raised so that when printed, they are black lines. Thus your print will seem more like the original drawing.

Study all the prints to check these points:

1. Is the drawing simple and graphic in its expression?
2. Is the composition unified and well balanced?
3. Is there a larger proportion of either black or white, insuring a variety in the dark and the light areas?
4. Do the lines and the textures express the subject?
5. Should unnecessary details have been omitted because they attract attention from the main subject?

Other Techniques in Graphic Arts

After the development of the woodcut in medieval times came experiments in other types of printing. A printing process, called *intaglio printing,* was completed by degrees. By this process, lines are cut with a tool or etched by acid into the surface of a metal plate of copper, zinc, or steel. Ink is forced into these lines and the surface of the plate wiped clean. Paper is placed on the plate and it is then run between two rollers. The pressure forces the paper down into the inked lines which reproduces them on the paper. This process is exactly the opposite of relief, or surface printing. Various types of prints, such as etchings, dry points, engravings, mezzotints, and aquatints are produced by intaglio printing.

110. SAINT JEROME IN HIS STUDY *Albrecht Dürer*

The climax of the graphic arts was reached in the sixteenth century with masterly engravings such as this one. The German artist, Dürer, engraved each line directly into the metal with infinite skill and sensitiveness, giving remarkable character and expression to every part of the print. Textures have been developed to the highest degree without any loss in the forcefulness of the drawing.

These methods, which developed at the same time as wood engraving, are still used extensively. For the creative artist, the graphic processes have always been media for expressing the ideas and thoughts that are more like drawing than painting. The richness of the printed line; deep, textural or light, delicate shadings; the quality that results from skilful use of tools gives to prints a depth and beauty that is characteristic of this form of graphic art.

A more recent development in printing is *lithography*. This method made it possible to print drawings shaded like crayon drawings from light to dark. Lithography is a planographic method of printing, so called because the impression is made from the surface of a porous stone or a zinc plate. A lithographic crayon is generally used for drawing on this surface.

By using special sensitized plates and photography, commercial color printing has developed tremendously. Fine reproductions of artists' work as well as posters, even as large as billboards, are produced through this process.

Silk-screen Printing

The silk-screen process, some historians say, was developed by the Chinese, while others say it was developed by the ancient Egyptians. Though we cannot determine its origin, we find that the method of cutting stencils for duplicating designs on fabrics was used in ancient times. Printing with stencils resembles the modern process of silk-screen printing. The stencil bearing the design is affixed to a screen made of very fine silk or organdy. The material is stretched tightly over a frame and the stencil sticks firmly to it. The design therefore becomes an integral part of the screen. Paint is then forced through the screen which acts as a very fine strainer. The paint can penetrate only those parts of the screen that are exposed, or have not been covered by the stencil. It filters through the screen and is deposited on the paper or fabric beneath. In this way an exact facsimile of the original design appears on the paper or other printing surface.

If a design consists of more than one color, a separate stencil must be prepared for each color. Each stencil shows only the areas to be printed in a particular color. The colors are printed successively.

The rapid development of the silk-screen process in the last fifty years

111. THE WINDMILL *Rembrandt van Rijn*

Rembrandt, who painted *The Admiral's Wife,* illustration 10, was a master graphic artist as well as a great painter. In this etching he shows us the forms, the textures, and the unique quality of his subject.

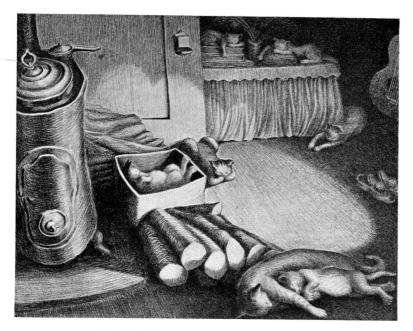

112. SIESTA *Wanda Gág*

This lithograph by a well-known American illustrator has great humor and charm. The artist's individual use of the lithographic crayon and her skill in developing a dark and light pattern that is full of movement lend animation to her print even though her subjects are in repose.

has been due to the great increase in advertising and its subsequent need for posters and various other forms of display in color. The silk-screen can be used to print on a greater variety of surfaces than is possible in any other printing method, for it works equally well on textiles, flat paper, cardboard, corrugated paper, felt, glass, cellophane, wood, cork, or metal. Silk-screen has also been used extensively in the fine arts, not only as a means of individual expression but also as a method of reproducing artists' paintings. Thus one of the most modern of the graphic arts serves a variety of purposes.

The field of graphic arts is a broad one because it includes black and white drawing, the designing of lettering and type, and the designing and making of all kinds of prints. The designing of fine books is also within the scope of the graphic artist. Acquaint yourself with the innumerable and beautiful productions of graphic artists throughout the centuries. Search for reproductions of their work in shops, in libraries, in galleries, and in museums which have a wealth of material for you to enjoy. A survey of the history of the graphic arts will give you a vivid picture of the various stages of our cultural development.

113. NIGHT SKATERS *Leonard Pytlak*

This silk-screen print by a contemporary artist creates a rich and brilliant pattern. The small, darting figures, weaving their way in and out of the busy scene, play the dominant role in the composition.

114. KITTENS *Elizabeth Oldo*

The decorative treatment of this subject is suitable to the technique of silk-screen printing. The cats have been drawn with humor and sympathy, and their arrangement is pleasantly and mildly active.

115. TRADITIONAL AND MODERN *Samuel Gottscho*

The beauty of bold, clearly defined forms is strikingly illustrated in this photograph. The contrasts in size, in shape, and in line direction between the various buildings are exciting, particularly the one between the church spire and the skyscraper. How many basic forms do you find?

10.

MEANING

AND STRUCTURE

OF FORM

IF WE HAD in our hands again the building blocks we played with as youngsters, we would understand them better than we did at that time. Turning a cube in one's hands, feeling its edges, its smooth surfaces, or trying to balance it on a finger would lead us to think about it. Even that old favorite, the rubber ball, is more than a toy if we stop to analyze it.

It is as difficult to recall our sensations when we first played with these toys as it is to recall our first reactions to color. If we watch a child, however, playing with building blocks and compare his way of handling them with the way in which an adult picks up these same objects, the difference in interest is revealed. The child tosses the ball or cube into the air, pats it, or throws it down. If an adult picks up a block, he holds it in his hand, turns it over thoughtfully, views it from all sides. He is conscious of its weight, its form, its texture, and the material from which it is made. The cone, the pyramid, the cube, for example, suggest to him much of the familiar world about him. Even such ordinary things as a basketball or a football, a cracker box, a tin-can, or an ice-cream cone have the character of one of the basic forms.

Basic Forms in Nature

The world is a sphere and everything in it can be reduced to some basic form or forms. The movement of the waves of the ocean presents a succession of forms; the rocks and pebbles over which they dash have a fascinating variety of form and color. Mountains, trees, flowers, and birds are essentially pyramidal, cone-shaped, spherical, or ovoid in form. Even

137

the human figure, although a complicated structure, can be analyzed, then reduced to a few basic forms.

Basic Forms Make Architecture

Shelters for mankind throughout the ages present these geometric forms. The Indian tent is a cone; the Eskimo igloo a hemisphere; the Egyptian tomb a pyramid, made from different materials to be sure, and found in different parts of the world. Throughout centuries of building, these forms developed in size and in complexity and have been combined to form imposing buildings: the temples, tombs, monuments, and public buildings of various civilizations.

Basic Forms Appear Again and Again

If we watch a designer of hats cutting or twisting a piece of felt, we may find that a cone or a combination of basic forms is the result. It is turned and viewed from all sides, for the designer is endeavoring to create a hat that is not only fashionable but at the same time satisfying in design.

If we watch a potter as he turns his wheel, we see how he shapes the ball of clay as it spins around, developing it into a piece of pottery. He never takes his eyes from the object being formed, for every touch changes it. Finally, he removes the completed piece from the wheel and sets it before him for study. He has created a new object that will play its part in the practical world.

An industrial designer, working on a plan for, let us say, a new automobile, makes a small model of his design. He carefully considers not only its function — that is, how it must work — but also its appearance. He knows that both the form and the function are part of his problem in design.

Forms Have Great Variety

Forms may be useful or ornamental, or both. They may be large or small, ranging in scale from an enormous building to a glass bead. The man-made world presents a vast collection of forms which contain other forms within them. Some of these are stripped of all detail and ornament; they attract by the simplicity of their appearance. Others are intricate or complex, and serve a variety of uses.

138

116. MODEL OF MAYAN TEMPLE

At the time of the discovery of America, explorers of the New World found temples and tombs with the familiar, basic forms used in combinations new to them. In this model of a Mayan temple, we find a design with each part beautifully related to the whole. Very little surface ornament has been used except on the highest part of the structure.

The second model, reconstructed from an ancient civilization, shows a tomb and its approaches. The former is a pyramid; the latter is composed of a series of connected, rectangular blocks with slightly sloping sides. The quality of both Mayan and Egyptian architecture lies in the variety, the relative proportions, and the repetition of simple, basic forms.

117. MODEL OF EGYPTIAN TEMPLE AND PYRAMID 2550 B.C.

We find in the industrial plants of today an ever-increasing complexity of forms needed to fulfil practical needs. Apart from their functions, the forms in this case are interesting for the variety of designs they create.

This huge, spherical form of metal, supported by concrete posts, is used for the storage of high-pressure gasoline. It is unusually striking because of its size and the simplicity of its supporting structure.

118. OIL REFINERY, TEXAS

119. SPHEROID TANKS, LOUISIANA

A head, a steel helmet, or even a cooking utensil can be reduced to some basic form. The workman's head is ovoid; his helmet is essentially an open hemisphere. The cast-iron muffin pan is made up of seven hemispheres. All about us are objects that provide opportunity for analysis of their form. How many can you find?

120. TANK CAR CLEANER

121. MUFFIN PAN *Early American*

Forms may be streamlined and so bring about increased speed in transportation. They may be so constructed as to offer more comfort and more rest to mankind, or more protection.

From the Simple to the Complex

As one remembers his childhood curiosity in examining and in handling a watch or a complicated toy, he recalls his surprise at seeing the detailed mechanism within the simple, solid exterior. Similarly, many beautiful buildings, pieces of sculpture, and other forms of art have exteriors that seem to lack all complication because they are highly organized in design.

In analyzing form, the second element of the art language, let us consider the harmony of the whole before we concern ourselves with the details or its mechanism. In considering the form quality of objects we must be prepared to inspect all sides, as well as the top and the bottom when possible.

First Step: Consider Proportion

What are the qualities that lead to perfection of form, which architects, potters, sculptors, cabinetmakers, and all designers of three-dimensional objects have striven to achieve throughout the ages?

Obviously, proportion might come first, since the relations of height to length and to width allow the widest possible variations in an object or a structure of any size. A pyramidal form may be squat, or very tall and thin — as far from the proportions of an Egyptian pyramid as from those of a church spire. A drum, a flagpole, a gas tank are all cylindrical in form, but consider the difference in their proportions! The Greek architects, when building their temples, followed mathematical proportions in forms, and their works still serve today as standards.

Second Step: Consider Balance

Any standard of proportion must include balance, for balance is a vital quality of form. Unless it is suspended, every structure must rest on its own base, but it can do so only if it is perfectly balanced. A structure which appears to be unbalanced, though it is not actually so, is extremely

122. PENNSYLVANIA TURNPIKE

A rectangular block form meets countless needs. A slight change of proportion seems to change its aspect completely. As a truck on a broad, modern highway, it represents power and efficiency. As a boiler, the same basic form becomes a well designed and utilitarian object.

123. BOILER *Gilbert Rohde*

Both of these industrially designed objects show the beauty of simple, modern forms into which a restrained and elegant curve has been introduced. The beauty of each object lies in its subtle combination of various open and closed forms. Notice that repetition of an emphatic line is the only form of ornamentation used. Both objects serve a practical need, and their design quality comes from a fine use of glass and wood.

124. DECANTER *Corning Glass*

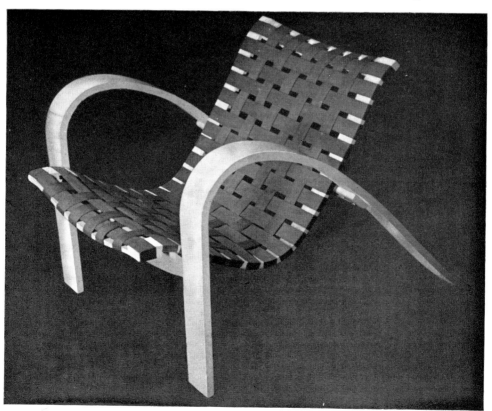

125. MODERN CHAIR *Albrecht Halbig*

126. BODHISATTVAS *Chinese*

Examples from the field of Fine Arts, such as these two pieces of sculpture, can also be analyzed for their form. The three compactly grouped figures of the Chinese sculpture and even the base on which they rest retain a basically cylindrical form. A piece of paper, rolled around the group, would touch almost every part of it. Notice that the base curves up and that the line made by the headdresses curves down to make the total form seem more compact. The vertical lines within the figure lend dignity and a spiritual quality. In contrast to this highly refined work, the bold cylinders of the primitive Mexican sculpture are startling. Yet both pieces show that their creators were concerned with organizing form rather than with showing realistic detail.

127. FIGURE *Early Mexican*

disturbing to the observer. A lack of balance, either of the formal or the informal kind, is as disturbing in form as it is in color.

Proportion and Balance Produce Expression and Character

When we combine forms that might be essentially based on cubes, spheres, cylinders, or cones, the quality of the result depends on the relation of each part to every other part. The proportions of a church or a temple, with the combinations of rectangles, of cylinders, and of cones in formal balance, produce the quality of dignity and of loftiness. Consider, on the other hand, the ludicrous effect of a tiny, cone-shaped hat on a fat woman or on a moonfaced clown. Here we find little of dignity or of formality, since there is an obvious lack of proportion and of balanced forms.

Linear Movement Is a Part of Form

The line, or linear movement of simple objects, is studied by tracing their outer edges with the eye. It is easy to see that the dominant line of an obelisk or a skyscraper is vertical; that of a bungalow, a train, or a boat horizontal. In contrast to these obvious lines, those in more complicated structures are far less easily analyzed. There may be dominant lines, those of the principal movements, and subordinate lines, those of the lesser and often opposing movements. A highly decorated Christmas tree still retains the vertical direction as its dominant line, but the garlands that are hung around it create new line movements of a subordinate nature as do the extending, ornamental branches. These less important line directions attract our attention and add to our enjoyment of the tree. Our eyes continuously weave in and out, up and around the main, vertical direction.

Basic Forms Are Not Always Apparent at First Glance

New forms can be created by changing the directions of the lines and of the proportions, by varying combinations of basic forms. Some of these variations are apparent and easily understood. For example, the form of a lamp shade is basically a cone with the apex removed; the dome of the capitol in Washington is a hemisphere, or half a sphere. It is clear that a chest of drawers is basically oblong in form. A dressing table is a little more complex. But from what form or forms is a rocking chair made? Its basic forms are not enclosed and they must therefore be completed mentally in order to perceive an underlying structure.

A New Field for Study

Whether made for use, or beauty, or both, the only way to determine the fundamental quality of form is by evaluating the proportion, the balance, and the harmony of all the parts to the whole. Here, again, personal experience will help you to become a better judge.

With form, the second element in the structure of art, you will be able to create designs in three dimensions. Are you ready to consider this field as a new one for exploration?

This building, designed for a tropical climate, is esthetically satisfying. The shape and the proportions of the windows are beautifully related to the simple, boxlike form of the building and create a vigorous dark and light pattern. The exotic foliage seems to link the structure to the earth and also to furnish it with an attractive and natural setting.

This building is so simple in form that we can readily analyze it. The simplicity and smoothness of its lines and forms are emphasized by the brilliant light and shadow of this sunny climate. The side that we see is exposed to the intense sun and therefore has corridors with small windows. The opposite, or shady side is kept for classrooms. The school is elevated from the ground so that an open-air recreation area, protected from rain and sun, is provided.

128. BRAZILIAN ARCHITECTURE

148

129. BRAZILIAN ARCHITECTURE

11.

EXPERIMENTS

IN FORM

WE HAVE BEEN discussing basic forms at great length. We have considered them both from the point of view of art and of use; we have begun to see them and to feel them as a part of our everyday existence. What can we do to make our knowledge and our feeling for form more definite?

Let us look about the room in which we are sitting. We see furnishings and other objects. They are forms, whether large or small, and occupy space. They are all three-dimensional. The very room in which we find ourselves is the largest form and contains smaller forms within it. Consider the desk, the chairs, the tables, the books, even ourselves. Everything we see is three-dimensional.

Experiments with Paper

Long ago you made paper hats, paper boats, or paper airplanes from a single sheet of paper. Intricately folded, it was no longer flat but became a recognizable object with a three-dimensional form. Would you now like to use a sheet of paper in a new way, a way that is simple yet creative? Roll it into a cylinder and clip or pin the edges together. Use a second sheet of paper to make a rectangular block that is taller or shorter than the cylinder.

Can you make other geometric forms from paper? Try a cube, a pyramid, a cone, and prisms with varying numbers of sides. Vary these forms in size, in shape, and in color, using not only black and white, but also gray, red, and blue paper. Secure the forms by pinning, clipping, or pasting them together.

Study Your Collection

Set all the forms you have made on the desk before you. Study them. Ask yourself these questions:

1. Are they distinctly varied in size? Have you, for example, a one-inch cube and a four-inch cube; an oblong block that is short and thick and another that is tall and thin; a cylinder that is short and wide and one that is tall and narrow?
2. Are the forms contrasted in value and in color? Have you, for example, a form that is black or red, and one that is white?
3. Do you know the names of the forms you have constructed?

Do any of these forms suggest actual objects or structures to you? Play with them as you would with building blocks; combine and recombine them. How many suggestions of the world about you can you find in them?

Further Experimentation

There are interesting experiments to be made in this study of form. Here is one. On one end of a piece of black paper place a small, black cube. On the other end place a white one of the same size. Do these two cubes appear to be the same size or does the white cube appear to be larger? Now place the same two cubes on a piece of white paper. Does the white one still appear larger than the black? Can you account for what appears to be a difference in size? Does it have something to do with the background on which the cubes rest?

Would you not conclude that relative proportions are variable and not constant? Beautiful proportions in form relationships can be achieved only when their needs are felt by a sensitive eye.

Another experiment: place a small, red object near one that is large and light or one that is large and dark. What effect has the combination upon each of these two objects? Does the small, red form appear more important than the larger one? If so, do you know why? Add any third object to the group, experimenting with its position in relation to the others. Does this third form seem to change the appearance or the importance of either of the other two? Is it not true that the size, the value, the color, and the position of a form are the factors that make it important or unimportant? The same factors are also important in achieving perfectly balanced forms.

Continue to experiment until you find interesting and unusual ways of grouping and combining objects that are different in size, in shape, and in color. As you work, consider each combination from all sides. Ask yourself:

1. Is the group interesting from all points of view?
2. Are its parts well proportioned to one another?
3. Does the group seem to be well balanced and stable?

Use Ready-made Forms

Collect a number of small boxes, such as matchboxes, pillboxes, and similar types of small containers. Include boxes that are round, square, oblong, and triangular. From this collection select a few and tack or glue one piece to another, constructing a complex form that is varied and balanced on every side. Try to make every part appear to grow out of its neighbor, so that the identity of the separate parts is lost. This type of design is called *organic* design. If, on careful examination, you find a lack of unity or compactness in your design, cut away sections of one unit and insert part of another one in it.

Color and Texture May Be Added

Do you remember from your first experiments how color can change the appearance of objects; can you make them appear larger or smaller, balanced or unbalanced in relation to other parts of a design? If you find that the color of any part of your structure interferes with the unity of the arrangement, you may change that color with tempera paint. Be especially careful to balance the colors, perhaps by repeating them in various ways. The surfaces of the structure may be varied by treating them in different ways, such as pasting onto them other papers or materials of interesting texture, or by denting, roughening, or cutting into them in some way. A contrast in textural effects may help to add appeal to uninteresting views.

Observe Each Step

At this experimental stage you are working very much like the scientist or inventor who spends the greater part of his life in rearranging and studying the results of his work. In the hope of finding something new or perhaps some simpler solution at each step in his experiment, he leaves nothing untried. The greater his imagination and willingness to investigate every kind of material and to use it in ways never thought of before, the greater are his chances of discovering something useful or startling and new.

Almost all the structures that you make will suggest something of the real and practical world. Put your imagination to work and you will probably see in the array of the work of the class some forms with which present-day designers are concerned. Even if you start without a particular form or object in mind, you may arrive at something that suggests a design for a gasoline station, a group of apartment houses, an automobile, a chair, or some other pieces of furniture. Possibly some additional touches might make your object practical. Therefore, continue to work on this first experiment to see whether you can produce a new design for a particular purpose.

Make Another Attempt

Would you like to see how well you can design something practical? Shall it be a new form of chair, a radio cabinet, a newsstand, a candy dispenser, a telephone booth? Whatever you choose to design, try first to consider the practical part of the problem. Before starting your design, ask yourself these questions:

1. What is to be the chief function of my production?
2. What are the practical demands that must be considered?
3. Is it to be useful or decorative or both?
4. What materials could be used for the finished product to make it effective both practically and esthetically?

Construct a Model

A design for a practical object, carried out in three dimensions, is generally more satisfying than one which is simply drawn in two dimen-

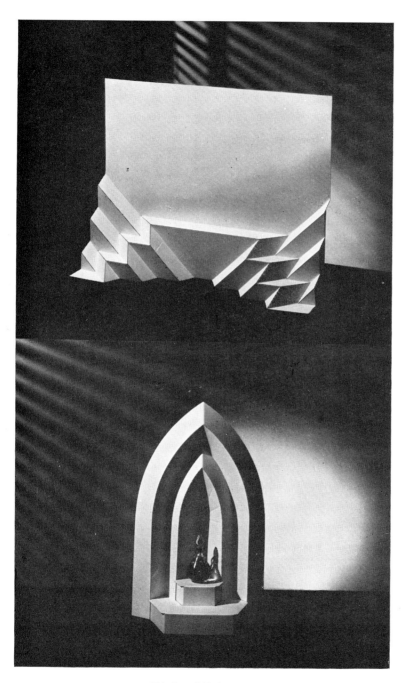

130. DISPLAY MODELS   *Richard Paige*

Beauty of form relationships and of unadorned surfaces distinguishes these little display models. Study them for their design quality, then consider what articles you think they might best display.

sions. For this reason we again suggest that you make a model to express your ideas. Plasticine or modeling clay is a material that provides a good opportunity for building and for cutting down. It is also semipermanent and an agreeable medium in which to work.

Take a block of plasticine and cut or shape it in any way that enables you to visualize the object you are creating. Consider all the aspects of the design with which you, as a designer, should be concerned. Is its form simple and well proportioned? Is it designed so that it appears both well balanced and equally interesting from every point of view?

If you find that certain views have less interest for you than others, it may be that the balance of the object is too formal. Experiment with it by adding some pieces of various sizes and shapes and cutting away others, working for a more subtle or informal type of balance.

Experiment with Free Forms

Take a piece of paper and cut a continuous and wavy line into it until you arrive somewhere near the center. Now turn and twist the severed ends, rolling the paper into some variation of a spiral form. Pin the severed edges to one another or to the paper at some other point.

The form that you have made is probably unlike any you have ever seen. Has it a flowing and continuous movement from one point to another? Do you recognize some basic forms within it even if they are not solid but hollow?

Can you find any possible uses for an object of this kind? Could it be a hat, a flower holder, a practical object of any kind?

Try Another Experiment

Fold a piece of paper so that it forms a rectangular block. Make some regularly spaced cuts along the length of a creased edge and at right angles to it. Try a different form of cutting along another edge, this time perhaps at a different angle. Now open the paper rectangle and fold some of the little cut pieces either backward or forward. Pin or paste the rectangle together so that it can stand alone. Does it remind you of a modern building? Do some of the cut pieces, because of the regular repetition of the pattern so created remind you of windows or other treatments of the outer surface of a building?

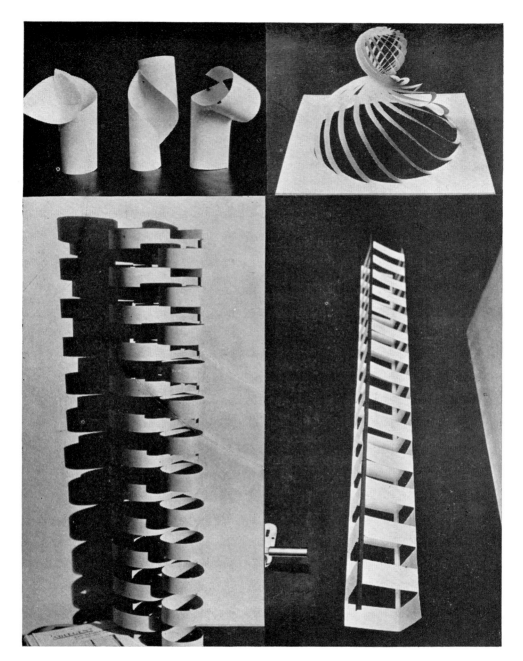

131. EXPERIMENTS IN FORM *Student work*

These exercises in paper construction illustrate the meaning of enclosed and open spaces. While you might find it impossible to imagine or to draw such intricate forms, you will find it simple to create them with ordinary paper. Each is cut from a single piece of paper which is then folded or twisted to create varied forms.

155

Architects use surface treatment for both practical and esthetic purposes. The upper building, an office and clubhouse, has permanent openings in the walls to reduce the heat from the glaring sun. Beyond the outside walls are the corridors and the rooms. The resulting surface is an attractive pattern. The lower building, an airplane plant, breaks a long and impressive wall by combining materials, by striping the concrete surface, and by emphasizing the doorway.

132. BRAZILIAN ARCHITECTURE

133. CONSOLIDATED-VULTEE AIRCRAFT CORPORATION, TEXAS

Do you not find that these paper rectangles are more interesting to you now than before they were cut? Can you see how an architect, in a similar manner, might plan a building with interesting effects in form, in texture, and in pattern?

Make a number of paper rectangles of different sizes and colors. Try to discover new treatment of surfaces. You might pierce two sides of one with small holes, regularly spaced, and leave the other two sides plain by way of contrast. Continue experimenting with surface treatments until you arrive at something which adds to the interest of the form, yet in no way detracts from the solidity of the main mass.

Group the Forms

Try arranging a number of these forms together on a large sheet of black, white, or gray paper. As you work, consider the grouping from all sides. Can you make it seem well balanced and equally interesting from different points of view? To do this you must be especially sensitive to the elements which affect balance of forms. Lightness or darkness; brightness or dullness; size and shape will seem to change in accordance with the relative positions of the various forms.

Cardboard Constructions

With practice gained in construction with paper, it will be possible to work with lightweight cardboard to create stronger forms. For the following exercises use lightweight cardboard:

Score some lines with the point of the scissors or the back edge of a knife and then bend the cardboard along these lines. You will be able to set these forms up for they will be like small screens or platforms. With gummed paper or scotch tape, several small sections may be fastened together to make more complicated structures. A series of cardboard blocks and an interestingly formed screen, for example, may suggest innumerable uses. Used as supports and background, they may serve to display many small objects, or they may suggest to you a stage and so serve as a model. You might even see the beginning of an unusual architectural design as, for example, a monument or a public building.

If you work thoughtfully and use your hands with skill, you will be able to create many interesting, three-dimensional structures that show beauty of line and also present striking combinations of color and of form.

Playful experiments in color and in form which use free cutting and imaginative twisting of paper can lead to designs full of movement and charm. The upper was called *Squaw Woman;* the lower, *Man with a Bag.* Although originally done without a practical purpose, they might well form part of an attractive window display.

134. EXPERIMENTS *Student work*

Look for Practical Forms

An awareness of form may lead to a great interest in it and may awaken in you the desire to examine everything you see from a factory to a football helmet, from a school desk to a concert piano. The artist who designs in three dimensions is one who serves mankind by providing for him all of the things that must meet his needs and at the same time satisfy his esthetic demands.

135. HEAD OF THE MEDICI MADONNA *Michelangelo*

Michelangelo, the famous Renaissance artist of the sixteenth century, carved directly in stone, an art which requires great vision and strength. The head still retains the natural beauty of the material, showing at the same time the marks left by the sculptor's tools. Renaissance art derived its inspiration and character from the finest period of Greek art. Comparing this head with the one to be seen in illustration 149, we realize their kinship, for both are characterized by restraint in pose, in expression, and in detail. This head is particularly remarkable for its beauty of line and for its clearly carved planes.

12.
SCULPTURE

MANY CHILDHOOD GAMES are based upon the love of making things. Although unconscious of this desire at an age when we made mud pies, erected sand castles, and built snowmen, we found it enjoyable to express our ideas in a visible form.

Pliable Materials Are a Challenge

Give a person a piece of putty or clay and you may observe how, almost unconsciously, his hands will roll, twist, and shape it. Soft material inevitably challenges our imagination and invites us to work with it. With this first contact there is naturally no thought of art. It is only when we begin to have ideas and try to express them that we approach problems that lead into the field of art and, in this case, specifically into the field of sculpture.

The Meaning of Sculpture

Sculpture is the art of *carving* stone, wood, plaster, or other hard substances; or the art of *modeling* in such pliable materials as clay, plasticine, or wax. In carving, a *cutting-down process,* the sculptor carves a figure out of a block of stone or wood. In modeling, a *building-up process,* he creates forms through working with pliable materials. Sculptural quality is attained when the carving or modeling shows the natural beauty of the material and when the characteristic tool marks and techniques of each process appear as a part of the finished product. For example, a figure built with clay and with no other tools than the artist's fingers should, in its final state, reveal his touch and his method of work. A design carved from

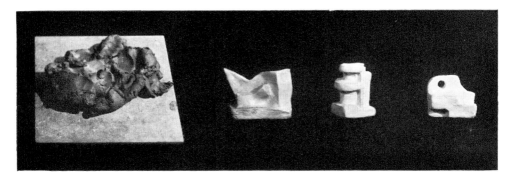

136. EXPERIMENTS IN SCULPTURE *Student work*

Starting with a pliant mass of clay and building up abstract forms in different combinations offer an excellent approach to the problems involved in creating sculpture. These students, using only their fingers as modeling tools, designed some simple and well-related forms that are interestingly varied on all sides.

Working in the same abstract way, a student found in her design a suggestion of a bird and she developed it into this satisfying design. The subject in itself is not important. It is the form relationship and the compactness of the piece that give it sculptural quality. Scraping the surfaces with a tool has produced the slightly textured surface which gives added interest to the clay surfaces.

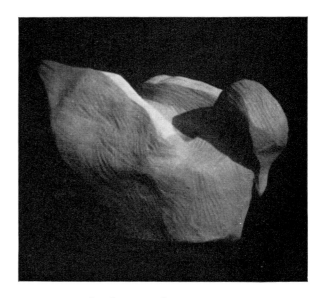

137. BIRD *Student work*

stone, let us say, should have large, simple planes and solid, heavy masses appropriate to the quality and the nature of the stone. The modeling process naturally makes more detail possible than the carving process since the materials are pliant, but the resulting objects should nevertheless have the same simplicity, the same structural solidity as those carved in stone.

Subjects for Sculpture

The minds of many people are stored with mental pictures of persons, places, and things, either closely observed in life or in pictures, or seen merely fleetingly. Actions of people and of animals, scenes and various forms of nature can be recalled to mind if they have made an impression on us. Yet everything we see or can recall is not necessarily a subject for sculpture, for all forms cannot be interpreted in the materials used by sculptors. Only solid forms without many details or fragile parts should be considered suitable subjects for sculpture. Subjects that are interesting to you chiefly for their color, for their delicacy, or their exciting action must be discarded if they cannot be developed into solid forms.

Experiments in Modeling

Let us begin with a simple exercise that will make clear what we mean by solidity, which is one of the basic qualities of sculpture. Take a piece of plasticine or clay; press and squeeze it until you have a mass you can hold within one hand. Close your fingers tightly over it, then open your hand and study the shape you have molded. As a form it may seem totally meaningless to you. But by continuing to work this mass within your hand, by kneading it, by pressing openings into it, by twisting and pinching it, by smoothing the surface, you will have your first exercise in modeling. At this stage the result will be simply a compact mass. It is neither hollow, nor loosely stuck together, but solid and changing in silhouette as it is turned about. Most important, it can be rolled on a table without any parts being broken.

A more advanced experiment might be this: Take a large piece of clay or plasticine and break it into pieces of various sizes. Mold them into three-dimensional forms, such as cubes, pyramids, cylinders, rectangular blocks, or spheres. Try various ways of combining these forms. As you do this, it is quite likely that you will develop a form that suggests an idea for a subject. One combination of forms may make you think of an elephant or a hippopotamus; another may recall the figure of a man bent over by a heavy weight on his shoulder. You may find it interesting to discover some recognizable object in your combined forms and to develop it so that it can be understood by all.

It may be necessary to add other parts to carry out your ideas, modeling them in the same simple, structural way you modeled your first basic form. You will find, for example, that legs may well be represented by short, thick cylinders, a body by a rectangular block or by a cylinder, a head by a sphere, a reclining figure by a combination of forms.

All parts must be firmly attached to the main mass. Additional material must be worked in and around the various joinings to make your design a completely unified whole. You must avoid long, thin extensions, such as pointed tails, thin ears, or any part that cannot be brought back and joined to the main mass. If your figure is compact, you will have achieved solidity, the basic requirement of sculpture.

Realism Is Not Important

When experimenting with modeling, you might think, " I should like to make a cowboy or a clown," then attempt to model a realistic figure complete with all its interesting details of costume. Such an idea is like wanting to make and to dress a doll. It has no relation to the art of sculpture. You must not try to illustrate a story or an event, or make realistic forms until you have learned what may be done with the materials that are used by sculptors. Ideas that you may consider novel or amusing in all probability would lack the necessary requirements of a sculptural form and should be left to the manufacturer of toys and novelties.

Consider Your Own Attempts

Have you reached the stage where you are uncertain of how to proceed? Try to recall your previous experiments in three-dimensional design and the conclusions you then reached. Study the figure you have constructed, examining it carefully from all sides. Ask yourself these questions concerning it:

1. Does it stand firmly and without artificial support?
2. Does it have simplicity and strength of form?
3. Does it appear to be well balanced?

164

138. CHILD WITH CAT *William Zorach*

A familiar theme with appeal to everyone is treated by this modern American sculptor in an unusual way. He has retained much of the original shape of the block of stone and has made each detail a solid, structural part of the design. The particular quality of certain parts, such as the child's hair and the base, have been emphasized by contrasts in surface finish.

4. Are the various parts well proportioned and are they related to the whole?
5. Do details take attention from the main idea or form?
6. Is the design of the figure attractive or is only the idea interesting?
7. Do you think that people living one hundred years from now will like and understand your work?

The last question may seem puzzling. Why should sculpture have a lasting appeal? What are the ideas that can be understood everywhere and at all times?

Universal Meanings in Sculpture

In almost every civilization sculpture has fulfilled the important obligation of creating forms and figures which incorporate ideals and beliefs of the state, the people, or their rulers. Legends of heroes, achievements of a people at a particular time, and religious themes all contributed subjects that could be expressed in a permanent medium.

Sculpture, to have lasting appeal, must be more than a picture in stone, wood, marble, clay, or bronze. Whether it is a small piece, designed for the comparatively limited space of a home, or a huge, monumental work for the entire community to enjoy, it must have a meaning that is inspiring and can be understood by all. What are some of the experiences and emotions which all human beings share? Our great poets, writers, and artists who observe and feel intensely all human joys and sorrows have found means of expressing them in forms that give them lasting, universal appeal. Can you do the same?

You may not realize that daily happenings which in some way excite or stir you produce similar emotions in others. Many experience the same series of joyful, exultant, depressing, or disappointing moments, but few are able to express themselves clearly in words. Perhaps sculpture will be the means of expressing your reactions to these experiences in a beautiful and satisfying way.

How shall we start such a venture? First let us choose some human emotion or feeling that we recognize as universal and worthy of expression in permanent form. Then let us consider how the human figure may be used to symbolize that emotion.

166

139. MAN DRAWING A SWORD *Ernst Barlach*

There is an expression of tremendous vitality and movement in this figure, which rests, however, solidly on its base. Barlach, the modern German sculptor, achieved action in his subject
by carving large and opposing planes and by keeping them as simple as possible. The figure,
though restrained in pose, conveys the feeling of an intense emotion. The artist left the marks
of the wood carver's chisel for textured effect.

167

The Human Figure in Sculpture

The use of the human figure to express an idea or to symbolize an emotion is very different from making a lifelike representation of it. Your idea must be revealed through the character and the quality of the basic forms, rather than by exaggerated action or surface details. Sadness or triumph, for example, will be represented more forcefully by a restrained pose of the body than it would be by a facial expression or by details of costume, for these are too indefinite and superficial.

In the language of sculpture, it is the inner line of a figure that expresses an emotion. To discover this inner line will be your problem. Your method of observation must be similar to that of an actor studying his part. He must observe how a person's body reacts to every kind of human feeling, for when he portrays a particular mood he must be able to make the meaning of that mood or emotion clear to his entire audience. In other words, he selects the essential movement, the pose most characteristic of the emotion he is portraying and he dramatizes it through use of a controlled gesture and pose.

Act the Part

With a group of classmates try to act out emotions you have often experienced and which you, no doubt, have often expressed without being conscious of your pose. Surprise, joy, curiosity, sorrow, perplexity, pride, shame, anger are all emotions that affect the pose of the body. Find the members of the group who are sufficiently imaginative and courageous to take dramatic poses indicative of these emotions. Observe the line of the figure in a crouching, tense, or relaxed position to find out if it suggests or conveys a definite meaning. This line is the inner line around which the sculptor builds a body. Try to visualize and to memorize this line, then to recreate it as the foundation of the pose you select for a piece of sculpture.

Construct the Figure

Secure a piece of plasticine or clay weighing one or two pounds. Divide it into four parts and shape them as follows:

1. With one fourth of the material, model a substantial, triangular form for the upper part of the trunk.

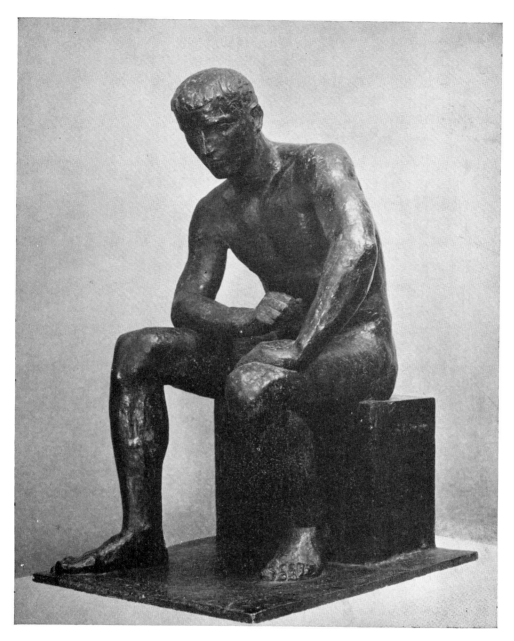

140. SEATED YOUTH *Charles Despiau*

This figure, cast in bronze, is an example of a modern French sculptor's work. In its restrained pose and simplicity of treatment it follows the classic idea of sculptural beauty. Notice how the columnlike construction of the human figure has been emphasized. The feeling of movement expressed is the result of an inner line movement which flows harmoniously throughout the figure.

2. With a second but somewhat smaller piece, model a rectangular block corresponding to the lower half of the trunk.
3. Half of the remaining material may be used to make two substantial cylinders for the legs.
4. The rest will be enough for two clyinders for the arms and a sphere for the head.

Join the parts firmly together, then turn, twist, and bend the body until you have the line you think best expresses the particular mood or emotion you want to convey. Your little figure will resemble no one in particular, for you are striving to make only an expressive, symbolic figure without any special features or details.

Work Thoughtfully

The above way of working has helped you set up a simple structure in a pose that may now be developed into a more beautiful form. To do this, add to the figure bits of material necessary to balance it and to develop a design that is interesting from all points of view. You can still bend or straighten the main lines of the body, twist or extend the arms and legs in the direction you find necessary for the particular pose you are endeavoring to create. Stop frequently to view the figure from all sides and to consider the following:

1. Does the figure stand, sit, kneel, or crouch without any further support, or does it fall over?
2. Have you achieved a striking design in this figure or does it seem too much like a doll or a manikin? If the latter is the case, perhaps you have not worked with sufficient imagination. For example, it is not necessary to keep the legs as separate parts of the figure. They might very well be either entirely or partially joined and so not only give better support and greater solidity to the figure, but make a more interesting design. Similarly, the arms may be joined to the body or brought together and so become an integral part of the main mass.
3. Have you turned the figure as you worked, designing it from all angles? Sculpture, like any three-dimensional object, must have more than merely a good front view; it must be interesting from all sides.
4. As you judge your work are you keeping other requirements of good design in mind? Are you considering the proportions of the various

Both these wood carvings emphasize simple, basic forms by their complete elimination of surface details. Both present sturdy figures, interestingly varied from all sides. It is clear that their creators, one of them a twelve-year-old boy, had long observed their subjects and were deeply concerned with making of them something fine and unique in sculptural design.

141. RURAL TEACHER *Unknown Mexican artist*

142. SLAUGHTERER *Mexican student work*

parts to the whole? The proportions need not be realistic, or natural; they should help express the meaning and might therefore be exaggerated or even distorted for that purpose.

5. Is there an interesting variety of forms? Perhaps the figure is still too much like the original blocks or like the form of a sausage and, as a result, lacks a forceful or interesting silhouette.

6. Does your figure show that you have worked it by hand and modeled it with your fingers? Have you given character to your treatment by relying on your fingers to build and to shape it, rather than by using bits of wood, a sharp pencil, or similar little tools that encourage a fussy treatment?

New Ways of Observing Familiar Things

Make a game of observing people and objects about you. You will never tire of this study if, from time to time, you adopt a new and different point of view or fresh interests. A little experience as a sculptor will make you more aware of the essential character of forms, whereas formerly you may have been conscious of them only for their color. Thus the old, familiar sights will arouse new interests in you. For example, a man carrying a heavy load on his back may interest you far more than you had thought possible. You may see in this figure the design which is the result of this man's need to maintain his balance in order to carry his load. Do you think that you could make a piece of sculpture that, by its line direction and by the distribution of a few well-chosen masses, would express in simple and beautiful form a figure carrying a burden?

You have watched a woman scrubbing the floor, a child holding a doll, a farmer cutting hay, a man working with a sledge hammer, and countless other everyday activities. Now observe them with new curiosity and interest. Try to analyze the typical movement and expression of the entire figure. Is there not a fascination in the rhythmic movement of people at work? Would not some of their poses be impressive in either a carved or a modeled figure? If so, let your mind dwell on the characteristic pose and plan to reduce it to a very simple and expressive form.

Attempt a New Figure

Begin again with the basic parts of the figure, putting them together as you did before, to create the main line of the pose you have chosen. Keep

143. CIRCUS *Chaim Gross*

The original form of the tree trunk is still apparent in this compact wood carving of the two figures. The artist, a modern American sculptor, found in this piece of wood an interesting pose for his figures, and by repeating forms and planes created a rhythmic design. The group is well balanced and sturdily constructed, and interestingly varied movement is to be seen. The grain of the wood has been skillfully used to enrich the surface quality and to add to the suggestion of form.

the whole figure as compact as possible. While it is important to handle your materials with some degree of skill, skill alone, as you must realize by now, is not enough to make a good piece of sculpture. An understanding of the nature of the problem of sculptural form, together with observation and feeling, must inspire your work. In judging the result, ask yourself whether or not you have caught the true character of the subject, if you have simplicity of form, and if you have handled your plastic medium directly and with conviction.

These experiences in modeling, and further ventures you may undertake in carving wood or plaster, are important chiefly as a means of learning how to observe sculpture and how to judge its qualities. Continue your interest in this field by searching for the best in modern and in traditional sculpture. Now that you have met some of the sculptor's problems, you may find greater enjoyment in discovering the wide variety of interpretations, of techniques, and of materials that form part of the sculptor's art.

Sculpture in the Past

In the past, sculpture was primarily designed to be a permanent part of public buildings. It was created to add meaning, dignity, and beauty to palaces, temples, churches, tombs, and other public buildings. In ancient and medieval times the sculptor and the builder worked hand in hand with the same aim: to create a complete and unified structure. Generally carved from stone, sculpture was considered an integral part of the building, rather than merely a decoration. The labor of carving stone, which often took more than one generation to complete, was an additional reason for selecting only the worthiest ideas to express. Remarkable skill and good taste were used in this work to produce sculpture not only inspiring to the people of that particular period, but equally stimulating and effective today.

Few names of the early artists and artisans are known. Their work, however, is proof of the culture and understanding of art that existed in those times. The problem of expressing spiritual ideas in a concrete form, such as stone, marble, or wood, without resorting to commonplace interpretations of them, makes the greatest demands on the artist. An attitude of devotion, as well as a mastery of the material, was needed to express the emotions that the mind and the heart had experienced. Any section of a Gothic cathedral will reveal the meaning of these statements,

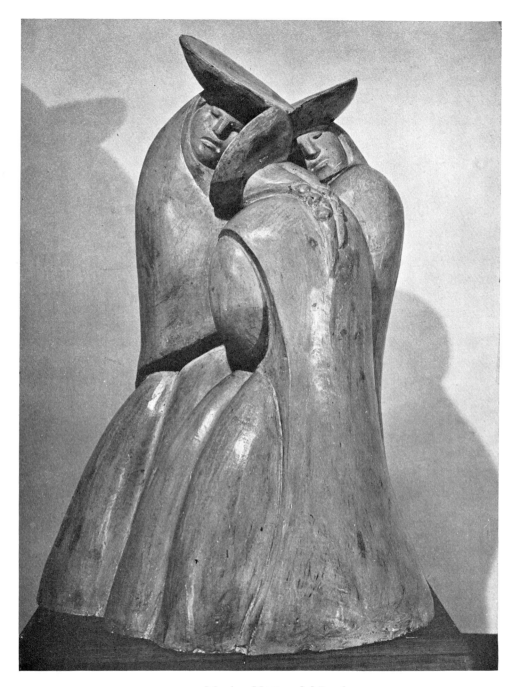

144. FLOWERS OF THE ANDES   *Marina Nuñez del Prado*

The dramatic pose of the three figures and the continuous movement and balance of masses make this unified composition attractive from every angle. It is interesting both as a design and as an expression of a mood. Each figure has an individual pose with different plane movements, and each flows into, yet counteracts the other. The artist, a South American sculptor, executed her piece in cast stone.

145. HEAD OF A BUDDHA *Northern Wei Dynasty, III–VII cent.*

The ideals of Chinese thought and philosophy are incorporated in this head. The artist has succeeded in expressing the spiritual quality of his subject in a material as resistant as stone. Its reverence and dignity are the result of beauty of line and of clear, simple modeling. Certain elements, such as the elongated and split ear lobes, were dictated by tradition.

Both of these pieces of sculpture retain the simple block or cylindrical form from which they were carved. While the Egyptian figure is carved from stone and the African from wood, they both exemplify the fundamental quality of all sculpture, namely, compact and unified form. It is interesting to notice that humorous subjects as well as serious may be found in sculpture. An exaggeratedly large head and an amusing expression help to make the animal humorous, while the formal pose and balance of the king give him a regal dignity.

146. KING THUT-MOSE *Egyptian, XVIII Dynasty*

147. HIPPOPOTAMUS *Northern Rhodesia*

148. HEAD OF A YOUNG GIRL   *Aristede Maillol*

The lasting appeal of this piece of sculpture lies in the way in which this great French sculptor organized the typical forms of a young girl's head. He used planes and simple masses in such perfect relation to one another that when the light falls upon the head, its seems alive. Although this head is in bronze, you will see, when you compare it with the stone carvings seen in illustration 135, that Maillol, like Michelangelo, derived much of his inspiration from classic Greek sculpture. The patina, or surface finish, of the bronze contributes immeasurably to its beauty.

149. HEAD OF ATHENA *Greek, V cent.* B.C.

An expression of dignity and serenity, combined with a simplified and beautifully designed treatment of the head in marble, makes this a typical example of classic Greek sculpture. Work of this period has influenced sculpture of successive ages. The artists of that time strove to attain the expression of an ideal type. This they accomplished superbly through perfection and beauty of proportion, and through the elimination of all superficial detail.

150. KING SOLOMON AND THE QUEEN OF SHEBA   *French Gothic, XIII cent.*

These figures are a permanent part of the wall of the Gothic cathedral, Notre Dame in Corbeil, France. Elongated and dignified, they create a type of decoration which is in close harmony with the sweeping verticals of the edifice.

151. MASK *Southwestern Alaska*

Many of us think of sculpture as something that can convey a feeling of movement although in itself it is immobile, or without the power of movement. To see all of its changing forms we must turn it in our hands or walk around it. But there are some forms of sculpture in which we find various parts that are capable of actual movement. This mask from Southwestern Alaska, for example, actually has parts which move and so create a changing design as they change their relative positions. A present-day American sculptor uses materials in his sculpture in such a way that actual movement of parts or even of the whole is possible. In this example of his work below, the petal-like shapes revolve sensitively in the current of air and present an ever-changing procession of plane relationships. The term *mobile* has been devised by its creator for sculpture of this type.

Sculptors, like painters, are constantly searching for new ways and new mediums in which to express their ideas. It is therefore natural that they should work in other than traditional materials. Stone, wood, and clay are still part of the sculptor's art, but the modern age has brought to him all manner of new sculptural media and varied ways of using them. Metal, wire, plastic, glass, and other materials, used with freedom and inventiveness, enable the modern sculptor to widen the scope of sculptural form far beyond early dreams.

152. RED PETALS *Alexander Calder*

for the long, thin, and expressive figures to be found there seem to have grown out of the very walls and are superb examples of a perfect union of intense emotion and a high degree of skill.

Another source of interest to us is the sculpture of the ancient Greeks. The sculptures on their temples represent the struggles and the battles of their heroes, the intervention of their gods, and their own wars. Although the subject matter is complex and recounts the stories of their mythology, the Greeks used these legends as symbolic of their ideas and ideals. The ideal human figure was created as a means whereby reverence and admiration for such qualities as prowess, courage, dignity, and poise might be expressed. Even in highly dramatic scenes the Greek sculptors showed good taste in carving figures in restrained and noble poses. This style has become a guide to us moderns in setting standards by which sculpture of any period may be judged.

The nature of Roman sculpture, on the other hand, is quite different. It is commemorative in character and consists largely of monuments erected upon the occasion of victories. Interest centered chiefly in showing real people in lively and naturalistic action, engaged in performing the deeds to be honored.

From fantastic wood carvings of the African jungle to the extraordinary totem poles of the American Indian in the Northwest, from beautiful Aztec carvings in stone to exquisite statues of the Far East, we find sculpture revealing the ideals and the beliefs of the nations, the groups, and the individuals that created them.

Our sculptors of today continue the traditions and the ideals of those who went before, yet each uses his medium in a highly individual way as a means by which he, as an artist, can create his own ideas of beauty. This is most ably expressed by the French sculptor, Aristede Maillol, who may be considered the father of modern sculpture. These are his words:

"In my work I look for beauty above all things. Philosophically, beauty is an abstraction, but in reality it is quite concrete. It is the thing that we do not seem able to analyze but that we can perfectly feel. I look for beauty and I know when and where I find it, and when I do, I am sure that others will see it in the same way."

13.
CRAFTS

MANY OF THE machine-made articles we use today were originally handmade. Books, paper, pencils, pens, and ink, now manufactured in large quantities, were at one time produced only by many hours of hand labor. We do not realize how much handwork was done for centuries, because we have grown accustomed to machine-made objects.

At times we find it difficult to tell the difference between the handmade and the machine-made object, for the former has been frequently imitated by the machine. Furniture, for example, although today manufactured in large quantities, still cleverly imitates the style of the handmade process. The very term manufacture that originally meant made by hand now refers to machine work. Careful examination of an object is necessary if we wish to determine whether it is really handmade.

All peoples have the craft instinct. To make a useful object not only practical but also beautiful has been instinctive to all mankind. The knowledge and skill for making handmade objects has been handed down from generation to generation. In silver, in gold, and in other metals; in clay, in wood, and in ivory; in wool, in reeds, in stones, and in shells; in glass and in fur; in feathers and in cottons, we may read the story of man's need to create, even though he use the most humble means and methods.

Qualities of the Crafts

How can we tell when a handmade object has a quality worthy of its craft, so that it may be considered a work of art? The skill with which an object is made is the first standard for evaluating the product. The

153. NAVAJO WOMAN WEAVING

Weaving is one of the most ancient of the arts. Localities throughout the world have developed individual techniques and types of designs, and have used the various materials available to them. The beauty of American Indian weaving can be even more appreciated when we see how simple and crude is the equipment of the weaver, even at the present day. The craft instinct of this woman and her innate feeling for design and color combine to make her products worthy of a great craft.

154. NAVAJO BLANKET

In early times the weavers of Peru who, like the Navajo weavers, were women, achieved excellence of a high order, both technically and esthetically. They were masters of a number of weaving processes and used them with great skill to carry out their designs, which appeared on all manner of practical objects. This symbolic figure, with its interestingly repeated light and dark colors, shows how designs may grow out of the very process which creates them.

The coverlets woven by American women of the Colonial period have never been surpassed. This one, which shows also the pattern of the reverse side, is sparkling in design and superb in technique. Traditional patterns, which grew from the weaving process, were followed with skill and fidelity. Such patterns were passed on from generation to generation.

155. PERUVIAN TEXTILE

156. WOVEN COVERLET *Early American*

Toymaking has flourished throughout all ages, and craftsmen never seem to tire of making humorous or unique objects. This toy, made of metal and wood by an early American craftsman, has the added attraction of movable parts.

The craftsmen of certain Indian tribes make these fascinating figures to serve both as household gods and as playthings for their children. They are carved from the soft cottonwood tree and gaily painted with earth colors. Tradition dictates their form, their costume, and their coloring.

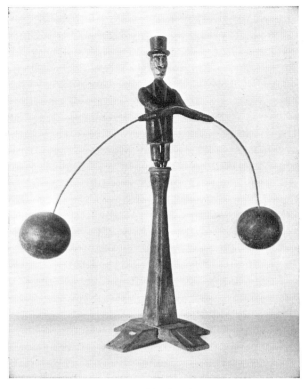

157. BALANCING TOY *Early American*

158. KATCHINAS *Zuni and Hopi Indian*

159. CREWEL WORK   *Antipas Brigham*

This embroidered design of the eighteenth century has an originality not to be found in the stamped, ready-made patterns of today. It was executed in a variety of stitches that were proof of the artist's versatility and craftsmanship. In the second piece of embroidery, executed by a modern craftsman, we also find an inventive and skillful use of materials.

187

160. THE CIRCUS   *Marguerite Zorach*

craftsman must truly understand his materials and his techniques. If the craftsman lacks control of his materials, his creation cannot be considered a good product no matter how interesting its design. Many handmade objects, on the other hand, which are skillfully made cannot be considered works of art. We have all had the experience of seeing some object, let us say a hooked rug, or a hand-carved wooden bowl, that is so exquisitely made that we immediately recognize the superb craftsmanship. Yet this same object cannot be considered more than an example of good craftsmanship if it has not the good design which is essential to any work of art.

A Craftsman May Be an Artist

When a craftsman in a particular field becomes an expert in the use of the tools best suited to the accomplishment of his purpose, his work shows a high degree of skill. In addition to expertness, the craftsman must strive to make his product beautiful in color and in form, and see that it has all the qualities associated with these elements of design. When he is successful in the accomplishment of his aim, and when his work, in addition, has character, the craftsman is an artist in the truest sense of the term.

Workmanship and Design

It is not necessarily the cost of the material that determines the value of the result. A ring may be of an inexpensive material such as aluminum, and combine originality of design with excellent workmanship. From the point of view of art, such a ring is far more valuable than one of gold or silver if the latter lacks originality or beauty in design. Always be sure to judge craft objects by the color, the form, the pattern, and the relation of the parts to the whole. The final effect should be one of complete harmony. If it lacks unity, it cannot be accepted as art even though it took a long time to make and required much patience.

Imitation Crafts

Among our possessions there are usually a few trinkets and souvenirs brought from various parts of the country. These knickknacks are often confused with good products of a craft. In reality, factories are flooding the markets with things that combine traditional or popular ideas with

With few tools and materials, but with ample humor, a soldier in a hospital entertained himself by making a unique and decorative mask using, among other things, a discarded brush, old wire springs, and can openers. Could you be as creative and original as he in your use of scrap materials?

This lively weather vane was made by a present-day New England farmer who carves for his own pleasure. Original and imaginative, it expresses his feeling about the storms and the weather he knows so well. His leisure-time pursuit brings him great satisfaction and is an inspiration to his friends and neighbors.

162. AFRICAN HEAD *Sgt. Winslow Anderson*

189

163. NORTHWIND *Charles D. McDonald*

164. POTTERY DRUM   *Zuni Indian*

It was instinctive with the Indian pottery maker to think as much about
the decoration of an object as he did about its actual form. The design on
this handsome coil pottery jar adds immeasurably to its attractiveness.
The modern set has been expertly planned for mass production. However,
there is marked similarity in the work of both craftsmen, namely, the
beauty of simple and well-proportioned forms.

165. DINNER SERVICE   *Arthur Crapsey*

inferior materials and methods of production. The only value of these objects is that in buying them the owner becomes aware of a certain craft and so becomes interested in investigating it; later he recognizes its best aspects.

Folk Art and Hobbies

We use the term *hobby* to describe the pastime of making things for pleasure and for the joy of working upon something in one's own way. Despite the struggle for food, shelter, and clothing, man, no matter how primitive, has found pleasure in making objects that are often chiefly decorative or amusing. Dolls, toys, models, and other objects in miniature that appeal to young and old alike would seem almost a necessity for everyone. Even when crudely made from materials at hand, they often express bright and amusing ideas, revealing the imagination and fantasy of the maker. The love of play remains with the imaginative person throughout his life. Masks and costumes for pageants, for masquerades, for fancy dress parties are part of this handicraft. In seasons of the year when the outdoor worker has less to do, we often find him occupied with his family in carving, modeling, weaving, or embroidering. Scandinavian peasants, for example, often spend the long winters in wood carving. The Hungarian peasant dyes silk for the colorful embroideries that his people have produced for generations. Sometimes townspeople will unite in these occupations and work out ideas for larger projects. Such, for example, are the "quilting bees" still held in some sections of our country. Their products are valued for the skill and imagination that produced the work.

All races, tribes, and countries display this form of expression called *folk art*. Some of these untrained artists possess a great capacity for disciplined and careful work. They have a feeling for color and for form which makes their products retain the qualities of their native background and heritage.

Watch for Traditional Crafts

Search among your own possessions or those of your family for handmade articles that possess some of the qualities necessary for a good example of craftwork. There are various sources from which you may choose. Has there been a traditional craft such as embroidery, or basketry, weaving, wood carving, or carpentry in your family for several generations? Perhaps

It is thought that this figure of Henry Ward Beecher was carved by a farmer from Indiana when that famous preacher visited his home. The self-trained artist, inspired by his subject, has caught both Beecher's spirit and a characteristic pose. As with all true folk art, this carving reveals the sincerity, conviction, and independence of its creator.

In many countries where dairying is the chief industry, the farmer has taken time to carve butter molds with which he stamps his product to make it more attractive and distinctive. A Vermont farmer carved these molds, using motifs that he knew well. They show his love of fine craftsmanship and his feeling for bringing beauty to everyday things.

166. HENRY WARD BEECHER *Unknown American artist*

167. BUTTER MOLDS *Vermont craftsman*

From Pennsylvania comes this earthenware plate. The artist used for his motif a militant, sword-waving and pistol-shooting rider on a spirited horse. The many curved lines produce a feeling of lively movement.

168. PLATE *Pennsylvania Dutch*

In the Colonial period of our country, lacquer painting on tin utensils was a popular craft. This dish is bold and brilliant in design and in color. Although the actual cost of the materials is small, the attractiveness and good workmanship of the piece make it valuable to its owner.

169. TIN APPLE DISH *Zachariah Stephens*

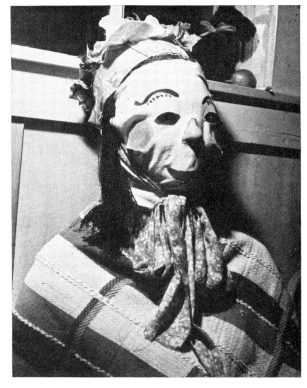

All of us have made and worn masks at some time or another. Here we find a simple and amusing one. While requiring no expert craftsmanship, it is a natural form of art expression that shows imagination and inventiveness in the use of simple materials.

170. MASQUERADE

This mask from Southwestern Alaska is thought to have been made for a traditional contest in which players, through use of humorous masks and comic gestures, seek to provoke laughter. It is expressive in its exaggerated shapes and features.

171. MASK *Southwestern Alaska*

at one time this craft was the trade or occupation of your people. The embroidery that your mother perhaps does today may be similar in design and in style to that used on the national costume of your ancestors. The weaving that someone now does as a hobby may follow patterns that were developed centuries ago in different parts of the world. Such crafts have a long tradition behind them and have inspired present-day craftsmen, both professional and amateur. Any examples that you may find will doubtless be enlightening and inspiring to others. On seeing them, you may come to realize the enduring qualities of good craftsmanship.

Watch for Acquired Crafts

Again, you may have learned another type of craft by following definite directions for making some article. Your first attempts probably showed only whether or not you understood the technique of the craft and had some aptitude in working with your materials. For example, you may have made a piece of embroidery by following a stamped pattern. After practice in executing a variety of stitches, you may be able to work out your own original designs. Thus, embroidery may become for you a means of personal expression and have genuine significance for you as an art.

A Hobby May Become a Craft

There are many other people who, throughout their lives, have devoted their leisure time to craftwork that has not only given them great personal satisfaction but also has eventually provided them with a means of livelihood. The whittling that most boys enjoy has developed, in some cases, into unusually good carving. The work of the blacksmith, who is still found in many parts of the country, has given many an inventive and creative worker the knowledge necessary for entering the field of iron work as a craftsman. There is perhaps among your acquaintances someone whom you might classify as such a craftsman.

If possible, bring examples of his work to class. Be prepared to explain the materials, the tools, and the techniques he used and to tell what is individual and expressive in the design or in the way in which the materials have been utilized.

Look for New Crafts and Adaptations of Old Ones

The craft field is extensive and in it today are many ingenious people who are producing new types of craft objects by experimenting with familiar materials or with those newly discovered. Cardboard, wood, papers of unusual texture are now being used to make objects formerly made of leather. New types of fibers, such as those of nylon, rayon, spun glass, and spun metal, are used in the weaving processes where formerly only cotton, wool, or linen thread was used. Sometimes traditional processes are followed and at others new ones are invented to suit the character of the material used. The expertness with which materials are used and the quality of the design determine with the new crafts the true value of the object, just as they did with the old ones.

Besides searching among your own possessions for examples of a craft, consult your friends and neighbors who, in the course of their travels, may have acquired some handmade articles. It will be interesting to learn why their owners like them, how these people came to possess them, and how these objects are now used. One article may arouse an interest in the unfamiliar material from which it is made. Another may reveal the manners and customs of other lands.

Arrange an Exhibition

Bring to class as many craft objects as you can and arrange them so that each piece appears to good advantage. Study them all, considering the uses for which they were intended and the way in which each problem in design was solved. Make your own choice of what you think is a contribution to the field of a particular craft and give the reasons for your selection.

Carry on Research in Crafts

As an additional assignment, search for books that describe some particular craft, that give its history, and show many and various examples of it. Compare examples of this craft made in one part of the country with those made in another, perhaps at different periods of time. Notice, for example, the differences between the weaving of the Navajo Indians and that of the Colonial Americans. Compare peasant embroidery with that

196

of present-day artists in the same field. Then, perhaps, you may realize that there are always new ways of using old techniques and materials.

After seeing work that expresses many ideas, many interpretations of problems in design, much skill and imagination, you may feel that you have learned a new language that will help you understand all people who express themselves through their handwork. For example, the handsome, fiery colors of an Indian blanket, hand-woven by the craftsmen of Nicaragua, may give you a clue to the character of the people. Through an appreciation of their work in craft, one learns to respect people of superior, native art ability.

Visit Museums

Many of us have the desire to travel, especially when we have an interest in art and realize that much of the pleasure in visiting foreign lands lies in seeing the art work of the people. Housed today in our museums are collections of crafts assembled by those who had the knowledge and keen interest to search for conspicuous examples of the various crafts. Frequent visits to the museums will reveal a wealth of beautiful materials combined with perfect craftsmanship. Our best designers and craftsmen of today study such examples. You, yourself, after seeing some of them, will no doubt be eager to improve your craftwork and make it more beautiful and more unusual.

Study Your Own Locality

Sometimes we believe that only in distant lands can extraordinary and beautiful things be found. Yet we may find the best objects near at hand, indeed right before our eyes! Almost without exception, every locality has a tradition of some kind of craft. Can you discover a typical craft in your own locality and find examples that are worthy successors to the early ones? Many local museums have complete collections from their own sections of the country. In them you may find pottery, metalware, cooking utensils, glassware, woven fabrics, agricultural implements — almost every type of handmade product. Be sure to visit collections composed of native work from your own section of the country.

An interest in the objects themselves will lead you to take an interest in the people in your locality who are still using their skill and their invention in a particular craft. Look up these local craftsmen and you will see the best techniques for using local materials, for these craftsmen are carrying forward the traditions of the first settlers of their particular region. From Maine to the West Coast, from Canada to the South, there are wonderful and varied sources of design in color and in form in our native crafts.

Learn, Practice, Then Create

Training in a craft you have received at home or in school may be the beginning of serious work in that field. With the ability that comes from practice you should finally be able to create with originality and so make things worthy of your chosen craft. Perhaps you have learned to do one of the following:

Model in clay or wax.
Carve wood, soap, or plaster blocks.
Embroider, knit, crochet, weave, or sew.
Work with leather, wood, or plastics.
Bind books or make jewelry.
Work with metals.
Make models of paper and cardboard constructions.
Make models in papier-mâché.

Begin to collect the tools and the materials necessary for work in your chosen craft. Be consistent in two things: keep your materials in the best possible condition; and always use them to create something beautiful.

The aptitude to produce beautiful objects develops slowly. To perfect yourself in a craft and to develop more and more interest in it will be immensely stimulating to you, your family, and your friends. Your own home will provide a background for the things you make and will reveal your personality. Thus you will carry on the traditions of an art that has been part of your ancestors' culture.

14.

INDUSTRIAL

DESIGN

WE ALL DESIRE to possess things, some of us because we honestly love and enjoy our possessions, others because we want to have more than our neighbors. The quantity of things we own is often made the symbol of our success in life; the quality is a factor we sometimes overlook.

Almost all the things we acquire are nowadays made by machine. Although we may not understand the methods by which a particular object is made, and may never see the machines at work that produced it, we can learn something about that object by studying it. Through such a study some distinctions may be made among the many things we have accumulated and some decisions reached as to their value.

Art Value Versus Money Value

The monetary value of an article varies according to the judgment of the person who judges it. One person may accept its market price as an indication of its true value, while another, because it appeals to him, would not part with it at any price. A third person might find the same object so unattractive and so lacking in taste that he would consider it of no value whatever. The true value of an object lies in our individual reaction to it. If we find it beautiful, or if it serves us well and for the time being satisfies our needs, then for us it has genuine value.

As our needs increase and we acquire experience, we may become better able to judge and to evaluate. We may examine an object with more attention to the material of which it is made, its form, its color, its texture, the construction, the workmanship, and its possible harmony with other things. Then we may ask such questions as the following:

1. Was the material used honestly? For example, a certain famous china-ware imitates a basket weave. Would you care to own china like that?
2. Would the object be more distinguished and beautiful if it showed the natural quality of the material, let us say marble, wood, or metal instead of being covered, colored, or finished with a surface that is foreign to it? Do you admire paper that imitates marble, metal doors with an imitation wood surface, or stone decorations that imitate lace patterns?
3. Would it be more beautiful if the form itself were simplified? Do you find that every part of it is related to the use of the object? Has the handle of a pitcher, for example, raised decorations which have no relation to its use?
4. Is the object really useful or is it one of the many gadgets which momentarily attract the eye because they seem odd or amusing?

By answering such questions one may realize some of the problems of industrial design, a field in which art plays a major part.

The Meaning of Industrial Design

Mass production makes it possible for many people to own identical objects. Can machines be made to produce objects that have genuine art quality? First, the possibilities of the machine and the kind of articles it can produce must be fully studied. An object that clearly reveals the character of the machine has an individuality that only the machine can give it. This object, then, presents the first qualifications for machine art.

The artist who designs directly for the machine and consequently for mass production is called an industrial designer. For this work he must fulfil a number of definite obligations:

1. He must plan an object that will function perfectly. This object might be a flatiron. It should be more efficient and easier to handle than any other yet produced.
2. The design of the object must result from the assemblage of perfectly functioning parts. Its beauty of form lies in the complete unity of its exterior. There should be no decorations that camouflage the mechanism.
3. The material should be recognizable. A metal pitcher should look like metal; a glass object should emphasize its transparency.

The brilliant quality of the glass makes this bowl unusually handsome. The designer concentrated chiefly on the relative proportions of the bowl and its base, repeating the spherical form.

An angular chromium bar and a glass disk are the main features of this clock, which was planned to harmonize with other pieces of glass on a desk. Its beauty lies both in its design quality and in the simplicity of its construction. It is apparent that the artist did not feel in any way bound to follow traditional forms or methods of construction when he planned this clock for machine processes.

172. GLASS BOWL   *Corning Glass Company*

173. ELECTRIC CLOCK   *Gilbert Rohde*

Kitchen mixers have gone through many stages of development since they were first invented. With each successive stage the form became more compact and unified, easier to use and requiring less space. Thus, both its beauty and its effectiveness have been increased.

174. KITCHEN AID MIXER *Egmont Arens*

Compact and easy to handle, this portable radio is a typical example of the work of the industrial designer. Leather and plastic have been combined in an attractive and practical exterior.

175. RADIO

Industrial design invades even the football field. These plastic helmets are lightweight, strong, and beautiful in design.

176. FOOTBALL HELMETS

Boxes may be commonplace in design or they may be as attractive as this one. It is constructed with a number of little trays inside, which slide into place as the box is closed. As there are no decorations, the box depends solely upon the beauty of its proportions and of its surface for effectiveness of design.

177. JEWELRY BOX *Gustav Jensen*

4. The material should be so used that it retains its own characteristics. A metal pitcher loses beauty if designed in a style characteristic of some other material. For example, a style used for an object of pottery or glass would be inappropriate for one of metal.
5. A machine-made object should not imitate one that is handmade. A chair, for example, designed for the machine and composed of possibly only eight parts, is far more fitting to machine art than a machine-made copy of a handmade chair with sixteen parts.

When these basic ideas are followed, the resulting piece of machine art can take its place with other forms of art.

Progress through Industry

Man progresses very slowly. Looking back in history we find that thousands of years of hand labor were needed before some of the simpler labor-saving devices were developed. For centuries the wheel has been known, and most of its many aids utilized. Yet only a little less than two hundred years ago men began to use the toothed gear, which is a kind of wheel, to build complicated machines. As the uses of the toothed gear multiplied, great strides were made in all industry. This progress meant more than just things for people to use. Man's energy perfected many materials, discovered new uses for familiar things, and found that there was often greater usefulness in an object made more beautiful. The industrial designer is concerned with increasing the beauty and the usefulness of machine-made objects.

If we review the stages of development from the humble dwelling made of clay bricks to the factory of glass and steel; from the ox-drawn cart to the modern passenger plane; from the early bridges of stone or wood to the modern suspension bridge, we realize that art and science go hand in hand in producing these and similar creations. If the result is to be an advance over previous forms, both art and science are needed to create objects in which the form, the function, and the material are perfectly unified.

The Past and the Present

Like an old family album, the pictures of the early stages of present machine-made products now seem quaint and even amusing. The early

178. S.S. PRINCESS ANNE AND INTERNATIONAL HARVESTER TRACTOR

Raymond Loewy Associates

An emphasis on long, low, horizontal lines and on smooth surfaces is characteristic of modern industrial design. We notice in both boat and tractor how interested the designer was in the total shape, rather than in its parts.

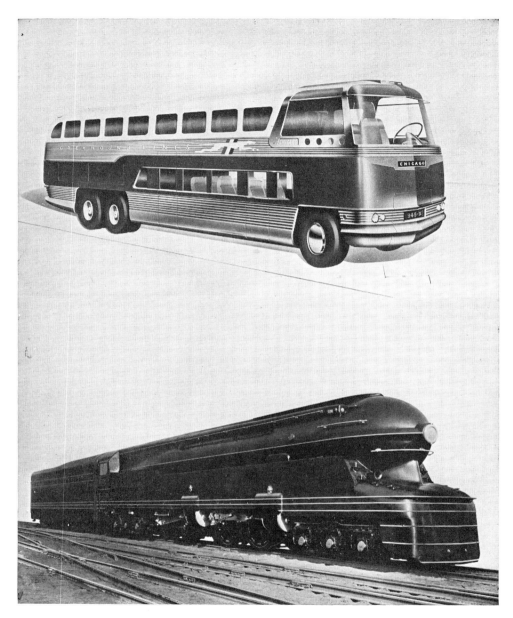

179. GREYHOUND COACH AND LOCOMOTIVE *Raymond Loewy Associates*

In the early days of machine transportation, inventors and builders were concerned only with the practical aspects of their problems. Gradually they became aware of the relation of designed forms to efficiency. Here we see examples of twentieth-century design where designers and engineers worked hand in hand to produce busses and locomotives which are impressive for their power and simplicity of form. The smoothly-flowing, horizontal directions suggest movement, and the forms themselves have been streamlined for speed.

automobiles, trains, boats, and planes seem crude when compared with those of our day. It has taken a considerable number of years to bring these machines to their present high degree of efficiency and beauty.

Let us stop to analyze the changes which have brought about the improvement over earlier forms. What qualities are the most noticeable in each advancing stage of an industrially designed object? How has a clumsy, complicated structure become so simple and compact? Let us look closely at a machine-made object to see if we can answer these questions.

Beauty in Machine-made Objects

Ordinary pottery mixing bowls made by factory machines are to be found in countless kitchens. Should we think of such objects as works of art? When we study one of these bowls, we see the simplicity of its form, how firmly it stands, how easy it is to use and to keep clean. There are no parts to chip or to break off. A ridge or furrow running around the bowl a few inches from the top makes it possible even for wet or slippery hands to grasp it securely. There is a pleasant difference in size between the base and the top and a fine proportion of height and width. The material of which it is made is a coarse, inexpensive clay that, when glazed and hardened by heat, is waterproof. Probably a simple band or two of a contrasting color is used to accent its form and to add variety to the plain surface. Thus we have in the ordinary mixing bowl one of the most useful and most esthetically satisfying objects in daily use.

Exercises in Selection

Comparison of objects is a good method for learning to discriminate between the beautiful and the ugly, the practical and the useless. Consider lamps, for example. Is there one in your home that you believe to be a good example of industrial design? It may be difficult to find one, for, while most lamps are machine-made, they are still generally designed in imitation of handmade pottery, hand-carved wood, or other handworked materials. Although produced in mass, they are seldom designed to retain the best characteristics of a machine product. Your search may be rewarded by finding a very small, very efficient desk lamp. Can you make a sketch of it for others to see, and can you explain to them why it is a good industrial design? Have you another that needs to be improved because it gives a poor reading light, or because its form lacks good proportion or balance?

Glassware is in everyone's home. See if in yours you can find a glass that is both practical and beautiful. Even one of the cheapest may be worthy of being reproduced by the thousands because it is fundamentally beautiful in line and in proportion, besides being extremely practical.

Report Your Discoveries

Collect objects from your surroundings that are worth discussion. Bring them to class and compare your choices with others of the same type that may be there. Choose from such varied types of objects as glassware, pottery, wood, metalware, and plastics. Include coffeepots and pitchers, salt shakers, flower vases, and kitchen utensils. There are also many interesting containers made of paper or cardboard. Consider various types of sewing boxes, tool kits and paintboxes, as well as powder compacts, cigarette containers, and matchboxes. All around you is a rich supply of manufactured articles to study and to analyze.

What Can You Design?

Your interest in machine-made articles and in good industrial design should be growing. Perhaps you would now like to become an industrial designer. Although the industrial designer is completely familiar with machine processes while you are not, the quality of imagination is one that you and he may have in common.

Imagination is the starting point for all designers. Nothing should prevent you from exercising yours. With practical experience and with training in the use of tools you may soon be able to perfect your ideas and to develop them.

Look at an old sewing machine. Can you improve its form? Can you imagine one that is more compact, easier to use, to clean, to store, or to move about? Can you also visualize a cabinet or a table for it that might serve other uses as well?

When the family goes on a picnic, all kinds of little boxes and bundles are stowed away in the car: food, utensils, blankets, sometimes folding chairs and a little stove for cooking outdoors. Could you not devise some container that would allow a number of these things to be compactly held together?

All shops have display cases. Even such varied things as candy, jewelry, and sporting goods must be so displayed that they can be seen easily and to advantage. Can you design a display case that is better than any you have seen? One that is lined with mirrors might help to show off things; or perhaps you have other ideas that you would like to try out.

Choose Your Problem

Consider activities in all fields familiar to you. Home life, business life, out-of-door life, and school life present many needs for industrial designs. What field attracts you? What object in that particular field do you use constantly? Perhaps it is a coffeepot, a baseball glove, a pencil case, a carpenter's box, or a make-up box. Decide upon one object you would like to design or to improve.

Make several experimental models for the article you have chosen. Be inventive in your choice of materials. Take wire, paper of different textures, clay, wood, soap, tin, or other scrap materials that you can fold, carve, twist, or bend until you have evolved a form that satisfies you. Use glue, adhesive tape, scotch tape, pins or nails to fasten the parts together. Be sure you indicate how the object should function.

When you find that one of your experimental models has definite possibilities, develop it in more detail. Make it as workmanlike, as accurate, and as strong in construction as possible.

You may find it interesting to collect pictures, sketches, or working drawings of articles designed by industrial artists. Study these examples to see if they are well suited to the purpose for which they were designed.

Houses Are Machines

Frank Lloyd Wright, a famous architect, once said, "The house is a machine," and as we look about our homes we can see the truth of this statement. Washing machines, clothes and dish driers, freezers and cookers make the work in a modern home more and more like that in an industrial plant. If we compare photographs of old-fashioned kitchens with our kitchens of today, we realize how important industrial design has become in the modern home. The assemblage of labor-saving devices within a home requires special thought on the part of both industrial designer and architect. Working side by side they have created, through design, a home that is a highly efficient working unit.

Modern architecture has greatly influenced industrial design. As the modern idea of a home develops, the separation by walls of parlor, sitting room, bedroom, kitchen, and basement has been changed by a plan that allows for greater flexibility within a house or an apartment. Instead of a number of rooms rigidly separated, we find spaces with flexible boundaries that allow them to serve a variety of uses. Modern industrial design in architecture aims at providing more light and open space in buildings. Thus we find glass walls, greatly increased window surfaces, even removable walls which allow a great amount of light to enter houses. Terraces and sun porches are so constructed that they are actually part of the house and make its occupants feel that they are living almost out-of-doors rather than shutting themselves in.

Pictures of historic rooms with formal arrangements of furniture, such as those of the American Colonial period, show that they were designed in complete harmony with the style, the purpose, and the manner of living of those times. Contrast them, however, with some modern interiors. Analyze each picture for the different proportions of the room, the effect of the arrangement of the furniture, the amount of space available for freedom of movement. We must conclude that the requirements of modern living are best served by the modern style of architecture.

Modern industrial designers have been especially concerned with designing furniture which can fulfill not one but several needs and can be varied in form to suit the particular spot in which it is to be used. In some cases furniture is actually built into rooms as part of the architecture. In planning such forms, the designer dismisses traditional construction and use of material and keeps two questions in mind. The first which he must answer is: What purpose must this piece serve? The second is: What material is most suitable for fulfilling that service?

Perhaps he is designing a chair. Through numerous tests he develops a form which is comfortable and may be placed in any one of a number of positions. Countless experiments with a material, let us say plywood, produce a chair that is designed to furnish both comfort and beauty. It may be adjusted to various positions and is light in weight; it can be manufactured at a low cost; the design seems to have grown easily and effortlessly from the material used. Although it departs from all traditional forms of

180. STORE AND SHOWROOM   *Raymond Loewy*

In the upper building, a modern store of steel and concrete, we find beauty and simplicity of design, undecorated surfaces, and an emphasis on textural contrasts. In the lower building, a showroom for tractors and trucks, efficiency seems to be the keynote of the design. The windows are unusually expansive and the wide extension of the roof provides protection against rain and snow as well as an unusual beauty of design.

chairs and lacks such separate parts as legs, back, or seat, and has naturally lost the quality of the handmade product made by a master craftsman, it is representative of a new art, the art of the machine age.

Design for Living

A practical knowledge of home designing is valuable for every intelligent person. Our homes should be experimental workshops, for there is no better place to test our ideas nor a better way for judging new arrangements than by living with them. Since you doubtless hope to have a home that is as well designed and as efficient as you can possibly make it, you will be interested in a few exercises to train you in the elements of home design.

Concentrate on form and space arrangement; use no color in your first experiment. Start by taping together some cardboards or pieces of stiff paper so that they form a little room with two, three, or four well-proportioned walls. Use a piece of gray paper to cover the floor space. Collect or construct a number of small cardboard or paper models to represent modern pieces of furniture, such as couches, tables, cabinets, and desks.

Arrange the furniture within the room, considering the function of each piece and the part it is to play in the plan of the room. Regard the grouping of furniture as a problem in functional space arrangement. A smaller piece of paper suggesting a rug may be used to help connect scattered pieces of furniture and folded pieces of paper may serve as screens to divide the space if you so wish. Ask yourself these questions about your arrangements:

1. Is the furniture in the place where it is most needed?
2. Is it well-distributed?
3. Could more of the pieces be combined in order to make the arrangement simpler and more unified?
4. Is the furniture lined up around the walls or has it been brought together to form one important group together with some less important groups?

Experiment freely with your arrangement by adding or removing pieces and, when necessary, changing their entire form or proportion. You might prefer, let us say, a round table to a square one; a longer couch; a lower chair; or more irregularly shaped bookcases.

If you have not already indicated the doors and the windows, do so now by pasting well-proportioned pieces of paper, neutral in color, upon

Designing furniture is a part of the work of the industrial designer. Here we find some which is in keeping with the modern spirit of functionalism. Its design is based on simple, geometric forms. The grain and the color of the wood, together with the stripes of the fabric, provide the only decorative aspect.

181. DINING ROOM GROUP *Gilbert Rohde*

An executive's desk in a business office needs to be designed for utmost efficiency. This one is unusually large and may be used by visitors as well as by its owner. The L-shaped form provides an unusual amount of extra and convenient storage space.

182. ROOM FOR BUYERS *Eleanor Le Maire and Charles W. Beeston*

the walls. Locate the windows carefully so that they are well spaced and well balanced.

Now let us enter the room with paint and brush, and bring it to life through color. Try samples of color on the walls, the floor and the furniture. Study each color carefully in relation to the color scheme of the whole room you have in mind. Your knowledge of color and its effects on the room should guide you toward emphasizing some pieces of furniture and making others appear less important. Even the rug may become a very striking part of your color plan. If you like, you might paste scraps of textile on the pieces of furniture to make their colors and textures more attractive.

Problems in Constructive Design

We saw how interesting it is to remodel a room, to make it more comfortable, more practicable, and more attractive. We have found that furniture, carefully arranged, can give far more service than is possible when it is placed without thought. Now let us consider new ideas in designing a single piece of furniture that can be used for several purposes.

You might like to design a desk that could provide enough space for all your special needs; a phonograph, a radio, or a television cabinet; a serving table which might hold a number of things, such as a small electric stove, a toaster, china, linen, and silverware; a wardrobe built into a room that could provide suitable space for every item of your clothing.

The Material Determines the Design

What material do you wish to use for your piece of furniture? Before making a final choice it is important to know something about how materials can be utilized.

Metal can be bent or molded, processed in tubular form, or cut and welded in many ways. Wood can be carved, turned, sawed, nailed, glued, or pressed into sheets as well as into strips or blocks. Wood in this form can be steamed, then bent and molded into shapes that are durable.

Modern processes have given new properties and new uses to glass. Glass bricks can be molded and formed into a variety of shapes and thicknesses of varying degrees of strength and transparency. Glass fibers can be spun, woven, cut, fused with plastics or melted separately.

214

While this early Colonial kitchen is quaint and interesting from an historical point of view, few women would enjoy working in it today. Bending, stooping, carrying buckets, and walking endlessly back and forth were necessary hardships in those days. A great contrast is this modern kitchen that has been combined with a pantry and dining alcove. It is planned so that there are only a few steps between each section. Built-in cabinets keep utensils and provisions out of sight. The rounded corners of the furniture add interest to the design and provide more floor space.

183. SCULLERY AT HARLOW HOUSE *Monticello*

184. MODERN KITCHEN

Plastics, of various degrees of strength and made from an amazing number of hitherto unused or waste products, can be molded into almost any form, flat or tubular, and can be opaque or transparent.

In this age of industrial design the study of art should include some knowledge of tools and of materials, more and more of which are available today. The chemist and other scientists are endeavoring constantly to increase the usefulness of natural resources and their by-products as well as to find new uses for them. Scientific books and journals can tell you what is going on today in the industrial field. If you have that great asset, intellectual curiosity, you will make it your business not only to read about the latest discoveries but also to seize every opportunity to talk with people who work in one of these industries, for they have an excellent, firsthand knowledge of the newest developments in the ever broadening field of industrial design.

Another Exercise

Use plasticine, clay, balsa wood, paper, cardboard, or any other workable material to construct a model of the piece of furniture you wish to design. Consider first only the practical features: the height, the width, the spacing and proportion of the open and the closed compartments, as well as all the features that will make an efficient working unit. Be frankly experimental and open-minded in your first attempts.

Arrange all the little models for a class discussion. Analyze each for its usefulness and discard those that seem trivial. Choose those that make a genuine contribution to economy of labor or to the compact storage of materials.

Now consider the esthetic qualities of each piece. Is it well proportioned, well balanced, and compact? Are any changes needed in its structure to improve the attractiveness of its outer form? Study each piece from all angles and note improvements that should be made.

Make a Working Drawing

When an artist designs objects that are to be manufactured, he must be able to make a drawing that will explain his ideas so clearly and accurately that the manufacturer will know exactly how to make the object. This drawing, which he generally submits with the model, is called a

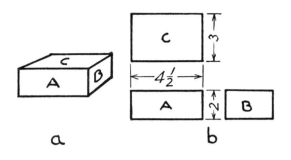

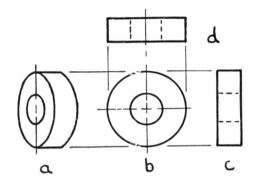

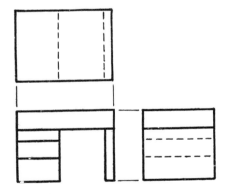

185. WORKING DRAWINGS

working drawing. It illustrates the model from three views: looking straight down on the top, facing the side, and facing the front. It includes all measurements and details of construction. From such a drawing the actual object can be made.

Let us make a working drawing of the box shown in (*a*) in the top diagram of illustration 185. This box is four and one-half feet long, two feet high, and three feet deep. Imagine that this box is placed on a level with your eye. A line corresponding to this direction is called the eye-level line. You should be facing side *A* since it is the longest side of the box and in a working drawing the longest side is always considered the front view. Draw this view in the lower left-hand corner of the paper. For this drawing, choose any convenient scale, such as one inch equaling one foot, and compute the dimensions given above very carefully.

Exactly above *A*, draw the top view, *C*, as it would appear if you turned the box so that *C* were on your eye level and facing you. Then to the right of *A*, draw side *B* as though you were looking straight at it. Here, as with the drawing of *C*, side *B* should be on lines extended from the top and the bottom of side *A*. This drawing is shown in (*b*). Notice that the size is indicated by so-called dimension lines that are lighter than the lines used for drawing the object. Dimensions are indicated at the bottom or at the right of the view. Give a dimension only once; do not repeat it on other views. Place the dimension lines outside the object and do not allow other lines to cross them.

A Second Working Drawing

Make a working drawing of a hollow cylinder, such as we see in (*a*), the second diagram. This form, in full front view, appears as two concentric circles, such as we see in (*b*). When turned to the side, it is simply a rectangle, as in (*c*). Since it is a circle, the top view that we see in (*d*) is the same as the side view (*c*). In order to explain that the inner line of the (*b*) view is not just a line but a hole, draw even dashes (– – – – – –) through views (*c*) and (*d*) to indicate the hole. These must correspond exactly with the position of the hole in the front view.

The third diagram shows a working drawing of a desk. Study it carefully, then make a working drawing of the model you have previously designed. Be sure to indicate dimensions.

218

" White Elephants "

Mass production has resulted in an accumulation, in every home, of objects that give little or no service. We dust them, move them here or there, giving little real thought to them except, perhaps, on moving day, when we are forced to realize how much of our valuable space they fill. Why not be as critical of them now as we are on those days of packing and moving? Our homes will be less cluttered, more comfortable, and decidedly more beautiful if we get rid of the " white elephants " that serve no real purpose. They are there for sentimental reasons or because we thought they were beautiful when we bought them. Why develop good judgment if we do not exercise it in our own homes and in our surroundings?

These objects should make us aware of the one evil of mass production. When commercial producers are reproached for flooding the market with " arty," silly, gaudy, and senseless objects, their answer is, " The public wants them." Consequently there is always some new piece of utterly foolish design to lure the thoughtless buyer. Let us all be firm in our resolve to select and to purchase only those things that have an art quality that is sincere and have also a real function to perform in our homes.

186. ROCKEFELLER CENTER

These buildings were designed to meet the need for a large number of offices in the midst of a crowded city. They resemble no architecture of the past. Their forms are the result of modern methods of construction and the functional demands they must meet. Amazingly tall, they tower over the skyscrapers of an earlier period of building. Notice that the insistent use of vertical movement emphasizes the height, and that the flat roofs, in many cases, have been landscaped as a part of the design of the whole.

2?0

15.
ARCHITECTURE

IN THE COURSE of a single day we enter and leave many buildings. How many of us ever stop to look at these buildings, to examine or to study them? We go down familiar streets almost without noticing them.

Most students think they know what their school looks like. They remember some unusual decorative feature; a stone ornament, a tower, spires, columns at the door, but does this mean that they know the building as an entire structure? Have you ever really looked at a familiar building and decided whether it was a pleasant or an unpleasant sight? Buildings deserve careful attention since they are an important part of the world of art.

The Requirements of Architecture

Architecture is the art of building. We cannot consider all the buildings that provide shelter or that fulfil other needs as works of art. It requires more than walls and a roof to make a structure that has lasting beauty. Yet a factory may be beautiful and a capitol ugly; a poor man's cottage may be more beautiful than the mansion of a millionaire. A building may be considered a work of art only when it is the product of the best thinking, planning, and creative powers of all those who contributed to its construction.

In order to be considered fine architecture, a building must have the same qualities of design that are so important in other forms of art. If a building lacks these qualities, you can judge it only for its usefulness.

In addition to excellent design, buildings worthy of being considered architecture should show the best use of the materials of which they are constructed. Brick, stone, wood, and glass can be used so that they are both functional and decorative. Just as a sincere person does not pretend to be other than he is, so in architecture we look for materials that, used in a direct way, clearly reveal their own characteristic qualities. Ornaments, carvings, and other surface treatment should never be used to disguise the actual quality of the material used.

Every building should be planned to harmonize with its surroundings. It should belong to its terrain, or the ground on which it stands, almost as though it had grown out of it and had become a permanent part of the surface of the earth. Too often we see buildings that stand out like sore thumbs, as the expression goes, because they are not in harmony with the buildings that surround them or related in character to the ground on which they rest.

A building must be designed so that every part of it is useful and functions perfectly. The interior and the exterior must be planned and executed in the same spirit, so that together they form a unified and consistent structure which functions throughout.

Architecture Must Be Honest

We are often astonished to discover that a building which is impressive from the front has an ugly, unfinished aspect when seen from the rear or from above. The so-called false fronts of many buildings are unfortunate attempts to present to the public a pretentious appearance, while the back and the top of the building are neglected. There are many ways of dressing up buildings to make them appear more important and so more desirable commercially. We should remember that superfluous decoration, particularly if it imitates historic designs, betrays a lack of good taste and, what is worse, a lack of respect for the art of building.

Architecture has been strongly influenced by the past. Architects often seek to keep alive traditional forms of building, even though these forms may not be in harmony with present-day methods of building. Thus, we have banks that look like Greek temples, railroad stations laid out like Roman baths, school buildings that resemble Gothic fortresses, and apartment houses that remind us of Moorish palaces, all planted in surroundings that do not harmonize. Architecture should reflect the life of the present rather than that of previous generations.

187. FOREST PRODUCTS LABORATORY   *Holabird & Root*

The basis for beauty in a design is the same for both modern and traditional buildings. The final test lies in judging the proportions of a structure, the composition of its parts, and the effectiveness of the whole. In this modern building, designed for laboratories, stone and glass have been combined to give the utmost light to the interior. This need prompted the architect to create a series of setbacks as well as to make a continuous row of windows for each section, thus making a practical requirement a feature of his design.

The Greeks built their temples to house and to protect the sacred statues of their gods and goddesses. Since their religious ceremonies were performed in the open, there was no need for windows. The severity of the solid masonry walls was offset by a colonnade of beautifully proportioned, slightly tapering columns. These columns were effective in creating a design of light and dark in the brightly sunlit land.

188. TEMPLE TO HEPHAESTUS AND ATHENA   *Greek, 421* B.C.

223

Architecture Betrays the Designers

Buildings of various sizes, serving many purposes, have been planned and erected at great cost of time and of labor. They may stand for generations and confront us with reproach, if ugly. The people who made them may be gone, but their work remains as a monument to their lack of good taste.

Architecture may tell the story of any race, its thoughts, and its ideals. It records the culture of its time because it is the direct product of man's way of thinking. The false, the showy, the imitative, or the shoddy building reflects the character of the people who built it.

A strong, compactly defined structure that is dignified and beautiful, that presents the best use of materials and is soundly constructed, that serves to inspire the community which built it, reveals a type of civilization of which its own generation, as well as those that come after, may be proud.

Examine Your Community

With some of these important points in mind, let us consider buildings in our city, town, or neighborhood. Study a railroad station, a bank, a courthouse, a school, a church, or a hospital. These questions may be asked about it:

1. Is it well proportioned?
2. Was it well planned in relation to its surroundings?
3. Is it equally beautiful when seen from different points of view?

Now let us consider the roof of the building in relation to its height and width. If the roof is flat, the chief emphasis will be on the proportions of the main mass of the building. This may look like a huge and clumsy packing case, or even remind you of a cigar box. On the other hand, you may find it a beautifully proportioned rectangular block or a number of rectangular blocks of different sizes combined to make an interesting design from all points of view.

Sloping roofs, however, provide an added problem in proportion. The angle of the slope as well as its extension beyond the walls are exceedingly important as factors in the design of the entire building. Spires, domes, and other extensions may make the problem even more complex. Whether the structure is a church with delicate spires, an apartment house with a

189. BELL TOWER   *Giotto*

This Bell Tower, an important part of the Cathedral of Florence, was designed by the famous Italian painter, Giotto. Towering over the surrounding and thickly clustered buildings, this cathedral was the spiritual center of its community.

For the people of Venezuela, the
tomb of Simon Bolivar, the great
Liberator, is a national shrine.
The dignified edifice, with its
unusually proportioned towers,
represents freedom from tyranny
to the thousands who visit it.

190. TOMB OF BOLIVAR   *Caracas, Venezuela*

This modest little New England
church tells us much about the
character of our early settlers
who built it. Simple, austere, and
precise, it could have been built
only by people who admired
those qualities.

191. NEW ENGLAND CHURCH   *Lancaster, New Hampshire*

heavy water tower, or a factory with an immense smokestack, its parts should combine to make a compact unit, completely balanced and well proportioned.

Let Us Probe a Little Deeper

Other considerations which we must take into account when we analyze a building are more complex than those of our first analysis, and they are more elusive. Go through some building, then walk around it. Can you answer these questions about it?

1. Does it show an interesting use of building materials?
   a. Are they so used that they have become part of the design of the building? For example, is stone used for the effect of its texture or for its color? Do overlapping tiles create patterns? Have materials so varied as metal and glass been contrasted?
   b. Is there a pleasing combination of stone, glass, metal, wood, or other materials?
2. Has the building a style of its own?
   a. Is it appropriate to the particular building, its needs and purposes, and to the community?
   b. If the style is derived from an historic one, such as the Greek, the Roman, or the Moorish style, has it been revised and changed so that it fits into a setting that is foreign to its origin?
3. Have practical needs been taken care of?
   a. Is there sufficient light and air?
   b. Are there adequate provisions for entrances and exits?
   c. Is the interior well planned as regards space for rooms and corridors?
4. Can you see in this building any suggestions of the personal or national character of the people who built it? Does the building show restraint, order, organization, and the high purpose of the builder, such as can be seen in the buildings of people who value these traits?

Barns Can Be Beautiful

When we recall the buildings that have impressed us with their beauty, we find that they are generally of the showy type. Is it not possible for a humble structure to be equally beautiful?

In almost every section of our country two types of buildings can be

192. VERMONT BARN

Space for storage is the chief requirement of a barn. Solidity and strength are fundamental rules for their builders. Though each of these barns has a different form, the design of each is completely functional, satisfying, and interesting from all views.

193. ROUND BARN *Shaker Village, Massachusetts*

found: moving-picture theaters and barns. Moving-picture theaters are seldom erected with the idea of creating a beautiful building. Their builders rely upon a lavish use of ornament and decoration, both inside and out, to invite attention.

Barns, on the other hand, are worth studying when the opportunity presents itself. They are absolutely functional and at the same time often show a genuine feeling for beauty on the part of their builders. The proportions; height, width, and depth; the slope of the roof; the size and character of the openings all have been carefully planned not only to enable the buildings to resist years of exposure but also to relate them properly to their settings. Frequently barns are far more beautiful than the home of the owner who has perhaps added to it until the original unity of the plan has been lost.

The site for a barn is carefully chosen and when built, it is adjusted to the character of the land. It is almost always visible, yet it is so much a part of its surroundings that it seems to have taken root there.

Now Consider Your Plan

We are familiar with various types of buildings that serve every town and city as, for example, the railroad station, the hospital, the post office, the city hall, the courthouse, a school, a factory. In the course of previous exercises you have become acquainted with basic geometric forms and possible variations and combinations of them.

Let us imagine ourselves architects concerned with designing any one of these buildings for a particular neighborhood. Consider these preliminary questions:

1. Is the building to stand in a large, open area, apart from other buildings or is it to be close to others? Will it be accessible from all sides? Will it be visible from a great distance?
2. Should it be totally unlike other buildings in order to show its particular character or should it be in the same style as the rest of the neighboring buildings? If the other buildings are already a mixture of every style, would you prefer to create a new and distinguished style for your building?
3. Does the purpose of the building in any way dictate the form it is to have? Is it, for example, to be a hospital requiring the maximum

Engineer and architect worked together to make this huge dam beautiful as well as practical. It is built of reinforced concrete and may be ranked with the most outstanding and ambitious constructions of all time.

This modern hospital has variety and freshness of design and, at the same time, it fulfills functional needs. Much of its attractiveness depends on the precise beauty of its forms and on the broad, continuous sweep of its flat, exterior walls.

194. HIWASSEE DAM *Tennessee Valley Authority*

195. LITTLE TRAVERSE HOSPITAL *Petoskey, Michigan*

amount of light and air, or a moving-picture house with a large central area with many exits?

4. After consideration of the purpose of the building, the amount of land available, and the character of the neighborhood, what should the height be?

Start Your Work

Take a block of plasticine and begin modeling the basic form that you have decided to use for your building. Consider it from all sides, turning the model frequently as you work. Use some instrument like a nail file or a flat piece of sharpened wood for greater precision. Examine your work for two qualities: proportion and balance. Add or cut away portions of plasticine until the shape is entirely satisfactory to you.

Review the Work of the Class

All of the little models, displayed together, will quickly suggest to you various types of buildings. Can you guess the purpose for which the designers intended them? In a low, semicircular form do you visualize a railroad station? Is there a suggestion of a hospital in a tall building that has wings extending from the center? Do you find one which seems to suggest an ideal apartment house?

Look at the models from all angles, with imagination and vision. Select those that have possibilities for further development. Suggest improvements for those that you find clumsy, shapeless, or without meaning.

The Next Step

These plasticine models still show smooth surfaces. Study yours carefully, choosing the best position for windows and for doors. Plan to group them in an orderly and interesting design. Use some small, sharp instrument and indicate them on the plasticine surface by outlines or slight depressions.

Select a number of the buildings that harmonize in character and group them into a unit, as a city block. Start with the largest buildings and arrange the smaller ones in relation to them. Move them all about freely until you feel that the arrangement is well balanced and equally interesting from all points of view.

Function Creates Form

We know that the form of a building is determined, to a great extent, by the use to which it is to be put and the materials from which it is to be made. It is difficult for those who are not architects or builders to under-stand the technical problems of construction, but we can all understand that a building should serve the purpose for which it was designed.

Let us experiment with a familiar type of building, a one-story house, in order to find solutions for the ordinary problems of living.

Plan a Home

Consider yourself, for the time being, a member of a small family. Where do you wish to live? It may be in the city, the country, the suburbs, or the seashore. The climate may be temperate, tropical, or arctic.

List the members of the family and the number and type of rooms needed to accommodate them. Make a note of the special features of the house which might be needed for their interests or occupations. For ex-ample, you might want a studio with an excellent light for painting, a large playroom for the children, unusually large porches for a family that likes to spend a great deal of time out-of-doors, or extra fireplaces if you are to live in a cold climate.

Now make a number of little sketches or, as they are called, floor plans of the house, showing various arrangements of rooms. Think of the rooms as blocks varying in size and in proportion but of the same height. Group them in various ways. Give the greatest amount of space to the rooms which are to be used by most persons. Indicate doors and windows by breaks in the outline of the room. Include closet space.

Compare your floor plans with those of your fellow students to de-termine which is the most successful. Imagine yourself entering the front door and going from room to room. Try to visualize the rooms in terms of comfort. Check your plan for the following:

1. Easy access to rooms, avoiding a railroadlike arrangement and long, narrow halls.

2. Enough closet space without cutting into the room itself.

3. Enough light and ventilation for each room.

Select your best plan and try another experiment with it. Erect paper walls about it by taking a long, narrow strip of paper and folding it at the corners indicated by the outer edges of the floor plan. Let it follow around the entire outer edge, whether it be irregular or compact, depending upon your plan. Pin together the edges of the paper strip where they meet.

Your House Now Has Three Dimensions

Now that your house has walls it is possible to see how it would look if your floor plan were carried out. Do you like the form you have created? Look at it from all sides. Is it well proportioned and well balanced? Should you change the floor plan in any way: enlarge or reduce any of the rooms or change their positions to make the house more pleasing? Would you like the walls to be higher or lower, thus creating more pleasing proportions than it now has? Make any adjustments which you think will improve the appearance of your house.

The floor plan may now be drawn to scale, using a scale of a quarter inch to represent one foot. The outer walls of the house may again be fitted around the floor plan, and the windows indicated on the walls either by cutting into the walls themselves or by pasting black or gray strips on them. The windows should be well grouped and should form interesting divisions of dark and light in the wall.

Add a paper roof, either flat for moderate climates, or sloping for a house that will be exposed to heavy snow.

Add the Finishing Touches

More can be done to complete the model house. You may landscape your garden space or, if you are especially interested in interiors, you may erect paper walls to separate the rooms, cutting little openings, in scale, for the doors.

Those of you who are especially interested in color might like to plan the color scheme of the entire house, inside and out. Recall some of your previous experiments in color to aid you in making an individual color scheme. Keep in mind the family group and the colors that would best express their various personalities.

Be sure to pin or paste all the parts together in a careful, craftsmanlike way.

Arrange an Exhibition

Arrange all the models for the class to discuss. Choose the one that

1. is the most pleasing in proportion;
2. seems to be the best balanced;
3. is the most original in plan;
4. makes the best use of available space;
5. has the best arrangement of rooms;
6. has the most attractive arrangement of windows;
7. makes the most individual use of color;
8. shows the best craftsmanship.

Architecture Is Building from Within

In planning your house you have discovered that the space arrangement of the interior determines the form of the house and, to a great extent, the design of the exterior. The modern architect considers the function of a building and how the space within is to be used as the starting point for his architectural design. Therefore, the exterior of the building follows the pattern of the interior and shows directly what the chief functions of the building are. For example, a modern dwelling in which the occupants desire a great deal of light and sun will reveal this wish clearly, for a large portion of the outer walls will be of glass. This wish differs greatly from that of a person who wants a traditional exterior for his home, a Tudor castle or a Dutch cottage, let us say, and at the same time expects a modern layout of rooms within. This calls for two plans for a single house.

A house, inside and out, should develop as one design. Remember this when you study buildings, analyzing them for their usefulness and their beauty.

The Meaning of Historic Forms

We recognize the nature of the ideals and the ideas of every civilization through study of the architecture of that period. Religious, political,

196. MODEL HOUSE *Jean B. Fletcher and Norman Fletcher*

Notice the unusual ways in which the architects have solved two families' needs for maximum privacy in an outdoor living area and for ample sunlight in the home. The overhanging roofs are a protection against rain and also lessen the glare of light in the interior. The simple geometric forms of the homes are relieved by the compactly grouped windows. Plants and shrubs are decorative notes against the solid wall.

197. MODEL HOUSE *Karl J. Belser and Karel H. Dekker*

235

198. TAJ MAHAL *Agra, India*

In each picture we have an example of the perfect relationship of a building to its surroundings. The Taj Mahal in India is famous for its formally balanced garden, which repeats the lines of the building. Although we see only a small portion of the modern building in Brazil, it is enough to show that the architect carefully studied the beautiful harbor scene and created an architectural design related to its individual character.

199. RIO DE JANEIRO *Brazil*

and climatic conditions, together with the materials available, have been the determining factors which have influenced the shape, the style, and the character of each building. For example, Egyptian religion dictated the preservation of bodies after death. For this purpose pyramids were erected that were to last for eternity. These monuments clearly indicate their function; that is, to protect burial chambers far below the surface of the earth. The massive temples of the Egyptians also reveal their ideals, their belief in enduring traditions and in the strength and power of their gods.

Both the character of the Greeks and the development of their political and religious life played an important part in molding their architectural style. An understanding of fine proportions and of restraint in the use of well-placed sculptural decoration, as well as a desire to achieve perfection in whatever they did, are clearly evident in their buildings. Greek architecture achieved a beauty that was a source of inspiration to generations of builders and designers.

The complex political life of the Romans required structures that could serve the public in many ways. Government buildings provided large areas for public gatherings. Aqueducts and bridges were only a part of their astonishing feats of engineering. Their architecture was dictated by, and fulfilled, the needs of a tremendous and powerful empire.

The rise and spread of Christianity not only brought forth a different political and economic life throughout all Europe, but through the intensity and the genuine fervor of its followers it also created architectural monuments that embodied all its ideals. Gothic cathedrals are supreme examples of man's ability to labor for hundreds of years to put his belief in immortality into concrete form. They rose and they transcended countless other architectural endeavors. Designed from a ground plan in the symbolic shape of a cross, wall, vaulted ceiling, columns, all lead to the principal place of worship, the altar of the church. Both interior and exterior of the Gothic cathedrals are imposing in height and rich in spiritual meaning.

Centuries of building after the medieval period produced countless variations of the Greek, the Roman, and the Gothic styles of architecture. Their influence is clearly seen in all building of the Western Hemisphere. In America, colonial architects broke away from European tradition by using wood and brick rather than stone, and by developing a style that grew out of the use of these materials. The twentieth century, however, is one of the most momentous in the history of architecture, for in this century mod-

200. INTERIOR, RHEIMS CATHEDRAL *French Gothic*

The immediate impression of this thirteenth-century Gothic cathedral is one of an uplifting, emotional appeal. The pointed arch and the ribbed vaulting express the fervent desire of the worshipers to strive heavenward. The inside and the outside are completely harmonious in spirit and in form. Stained glass windows, superb in craftsmanship and in color, contribute to a luminous interior.

238

201. AMIENS CATHEDRAL *French Gothic*

Sculptural decoration plays an important part in the design of this famous cathedral. It enriches the portals and adds immeasurably to the textural quality of the entire surface. Our impression is one of spiritual and architectural unity. The richness of detail and the recessed areas create a brilliant pattern of dark and light.

239

ern architecture was born. It departed from traditional styles of construction and gradually freed us from blind worship of the past, so that our modern buildings, both public and private, are the product of clear and straightforward thinking, of a high degree of technical knowledge, and above all, of sound esthetic judgment. The new era of modern architecture is striking proof of the power of art to make a substantial contribution to the welfare and happiness of mankind.

Architecture Identifies Its Builders

If you know something of the life and character of a nation, you will be able to see a relation between its architecture and the aims and ideals of its builders. People differ greatly. Some prize stability and order. They seek beauty and wish to express it in the structures which they erect. Others, who are materialistic and strictly practical, are in no way concerned with the esthetics of building. Then there are those who express their hope and belief in a spiritual world by building cathedrals, temples, and other places of worship. Men have built and will continue to build in different ways, for in their interest, their ability, and their patience they vary greatly. It took generations to complete a cathedral; endless skill and devotion made every part of these structures a work of art. Today we expect few of our buildings to outlive a generation and its needs. This idea makes for progress, but it also produces careless building. Since this is one of the greatest eras of building, we, as a nation, must see to it that our architecture expresses our dignity, our strength, and our ideals.

16.

COMMUNITY

PLANNING

HAVE YOU EVER TAKEN an airplane ride? Our world, seen from above, is fascinating. A surprising design of fields and forests, of roads and rivers, of clusters of houses and towns makes an enchanting pattern. Boats, trains, and cars, mere specks on the surface, follow their appointed paths, and the whole picture is that of a busy and well-organized miniature world.

But when we return to earth, the scene changes. The pattern is no longer clear, nor does it seem to be an organized whole. Even our own city block or neighborhood is often without a consistent plan. We accept our surroundings without much thought because we are accustomed to them, and it never occurs to us that they might be changed.

In fact, it occurs to very few people that a change could be made in the plan of our towns or cities. We move into a neighborhood because we like it, or we move out of one, if possible, when it no longer pleases us. To destroy and to rebuild houses, to widen or to straighten streets, to open spaces in crowded sections, or to change dangerous traffic lanes seem far too difficult to do.

Communities Must Be Planned

It requires courage and foresight to plan a change that will affect the lives of many persons. Community planning is an art that requires the best thinking, the clearest judgment, and the most sympathetic understanding of man's need for physical and spiritual comfort.

The desire to live in beautiful, congenial surroundings grows out of the same impulse that drives man to improve and to beautify everything that he makes and owns. But to make our surroundings beautiful cannot be considered merely an individual problem. While a few people can accomplish this because they have the means to do so, the vast majority of us must depend upon concerted effort; each one of us must share in the enterprise, in the plan, and in its execution. To say, or to think, " Oh, most of the time I just exist, except for the few weeks I get away to the country," is evidence of an attitude that is human but at the same time uncooperative.

Planning a Community

The ideal way to plan a community is to start in an undeveloped section which is richly endowed by nature. Many fine communities have been planned and successfully developed in this way. Planned communities, the result of the work of private enterprise, federal government, or town, county, or local groups interested in improving their own region may be found in various parts of our country. Four communities, called Greenbelt Towns, located in Indiana, Wisconsin, Ohio, and Maryland, were built by the Resettlement Administration. They are different from most towns because they did not grow at random but were completely planned in every detail long before their construction was begun. Streets, schools, utility systems, stores, parks, and dwelling areas were all designed for the greatest possible comfort and efficiency. In these towns there are no slums or run-down sections nor will there be any in the future. Each is surrounded by a protecting " greenbelt " of parks, farms, and forests to keep undesirable developments from crowding the community, and the plan of each town will prevent such growth within the village limits.

The Greenbelt Towns were among the first completely planned communities built in the United States. Chatham Village, in a section of Pittsburgh, is another well-planned private development, as is Radburn, New Jersey, a town with more green spaces and fewer streets than are found in the average suburb. The town of Hill, in New Hampshire, is worthy of study; Baldwin Hills Village, in Los Angeles, has been described as " probably the most seriously progressive experiment in home building by private enterprise since Radburn was started a number of years ago."

However, the most vital need for community planning lies in the heart of our cities, in sections where hundreds of thousands of people are herded together without sufficient space, light, or air. These are the districts in greatest need. Can community plans for sections such as these be

242

202. NARDEN *Holland*

The air-view of this town reveals its striking, starlike form. The orderly arrangement of surrounding fields and trees helps to set it off like a well-cut jewel in a beautiful setting.

203. GREENBELT *Maryland*

This is one of the first United States Government projects undertaken to provide a community of low-cost homes. It is located about twelve miles from Washington, D. C. An airplane view reveals the surrounding belt of woodland which prevents this community from developing in an unplanned fashion.

carried out? They can, but only with the help of each and every one of us. Some have the knowledge, the experience, and the wisdom to plan; others have the necessary strength and power to see that plans are carried out, even over a long period of time. Even more important, are the people who, because of their steadfast belief in what is beautiful and thoughtfully planned, will not only refuse to accept chaotic, ugly surroundings, but will indeed work with every means at their disposal to forward a plan that concerns the welfare of all.

Basic Requirements for Living

What are the requirements for happy, congenial life in a community? Is there an underlying pattern that could secure for each of us a minimum of discomfort and frustration, a maximum of comfort and of beauty with its consequent freedom of spirit? The basic requirements for a fine community plan might be reached after considering the following questions. Think them over; discuss them with your classmates, your friends, and your family.

1. Should a limit be placed upon the number of people who can live within a stated area?
2. Should a community be self-sufficient? That is, should each have its own civic center, its schools, its playgrounds and recreation centers, movies and theaters, and, especially, its means of livelihood near at hand, within walking distance if possible?
3. Should main thoroughfares be planned so that they lead around rather than through the heart of the community?
4. Should public places, such as those for entertainment, for buying, for selling, for eating, and for similar purposes be kept within fixed areas?
5. Should the whole be planned so that not only each person in the family group but in the entire community as well can find comfort, satisfaction, and pleasure in everyday existence?

Your answers to these questions provide the starting point for your own work in this field of art that is the most important you have attempted so far. Should we try to plan for a community that will benefit each of its inhabitants? If you are interested, we suggest that you start in the most direct way possible: by considering your own immediate neighborhood.

204. CIRCULAR VILLAGE

This European rural town was arranged in the curved plan derived from the early medieval system. The main roads flank the town, giving the inhabitants easy access to outlying farmlands. The lower town, arranged on either side of a wide road, illustrates the ribbon system which is practical for rural sections.

205. STREET VILLAGE, RIBBON SYSTEM

206. REAL ESTATE DEVELOPMENT *Queens, New York City*

This so-called development resembles an array of traps, so identical that each owner can scarcely distinguish his own home. The narrow passageways between buildings are dark and useless; neither front nor backyard affords privacy. There is an obvious lack of sufficient light and air. In the lower photograph, the community in the foreground shows an interestingly curved arrangement of one and two-story houses. Each building has been provided with a generous amount of surrounding space. Compare this with the closely packed rows of houses to be seen above.

207. HILL CREEK *Philadelphia, Pennsylvania*

Scenes such as this are only too common in our cities. Compare this one with the photograph below which shows the same section after a community project was completed there. Erected in 1938, within regulations determining the height and form of the buildings, sufficient space, air, and sunlight were provided.

208. WILLIAMSBURG   *New York City*

209. WILLIAMSBURG HOUSING   *New York City*

Explore Your Own Community

Examine and explore your neighborhood. Acquaint yourself with its physical characteristics; the background and the interests of its inhabitants; their means of livelihood. In terms of these necessary considerations, answer the following:

1. Is the section rural or urban? Is it an agricultural or an industrial center? What is the chief occupation of its residents?
2. Has every home adequate light, air, and space?
3. Has the community its own places of worship, its schools, its civic, shopping, and recreation centers?
4. Is it, on the whole, a pleasant neighborhood in which to live? Are the buildings, parks, and views beautiful and fitted to the purpose for which they were planned? Have individuals privacy when they wish it?
5. Do main traffic arteries run through the streets so that walking and playing are perilous, or are the streets by-lanes, through which only essential community traffic passes?

The Meaning of Community Spirit

Consideration of an ideal community leads us to analyze the benefits that would be derived from living in one that was ideal. It is surely clear that harmony of living leads to personal happiness, to mutual trust and friendliness. A feeling of comfort and security, as well as loyalty to one's neighbors and associates, is the natural result of strong home ties. In such an environment each one is prompted to do his best and most creative work. From a stimulus as this can come a true appreciation of the part that art plays in making our lives richer, healthier, and therefore, fuller and more beautiful.

For the first time we have mentioned the word " art " in connection with the community plan. But we all know that art is a force that can shape our lives and enable us to fulfill our destinies. Your experience in art and your knowledge of its relation to everyday living will be put to the test if you embark on a problem that affects not only your life but also that of your fellowmen. Are you interested in seeing how your knowledge of art can be used to benefit your entire community?

Map Out Your Own Community

You must work with others to secure a clear picture of your community. Take a large sheet of wrapping or detail paper and spread it out on a table. Draw in the boundaries of your community. Next add the important physical features, such as rivers, lakes, mountains, or swampy sections. Then show the main traffic arteries, and, finally, each block or square of dwellings.

Now for a piece of personal research. Each student should select a small part of his community for a detailed report. Go to that section and study it, armed with your sketchbook. Make a sketch that shows clearly the number of buildings in the block. Indicate by captions the use of each building, such as factory, private dwelling, apartment house, theater, store, or garage. Below this caption note the number of stories in each building. As a final piece of volunteer work, try to estimate the number of people who live in a particular block or square.

Then in class transfer all the information about your section to the large map. When each part of the map has been developed, we suggest that you use crayons to clarify certain features. You might indicate water by light blue, public buildings by red, and parks by green. All residences might be colored yellow. Now you are ready to analyze this community as a whole.

Study Your Map

1. Are the residential sections too congested? From your figures you can estimate the number of people who live in any given area.
2. Are the public buildings so situated that they are within walking distance for all; that is, are they reasonably centered, or are they at the far end of the community?
3. Are there enough large, open areas — parks, lawns, trees, playgrounds, and the like — or are there only a small number scattered about?
4. Is there much waste space that could be built up or used to advantage for parks or for public buildings?
5. Are factories or other industrial buildings located where they spoil the section for the residents?

Make a New Map

Through analysis of your community you have discovered its defects. It must be clear to you that a city or any section of it, or a town without an underlying plan followed for the advantage of the entire group, benefits only a small part of the inhabitants. Perhaps you are discouraged with what you see and wonder, at this time, how anything can be done to improve your community. Many things can be accomplished if you have good ideas and the will power to see them developed. So, first of all, put your ideas on paper in order to get them into concrete form.

Each of you should now improve the design of your community. This may be done on a smaller scale and in far less detail than on the first map you worked on. From your first study of the community you know the conditions that need correcting. Using color, make a plan and show on it where you would place public buildings, parks, industrial and residential sections. Try to avoid crowding large groups of people together and try to provide adequate light, air, and open, green spaces for all. Do you think it necessary to widen certain traffic lanes or to eliminate some? Be especially careful to provide safe and easy passage to schools and to play-grounds for children.

Compare Plans

Look at all the plans made by your classmates and discuss them thoroughly. Consider each idea offered. Allow each student the opportunity to discuss the arrangement he thinks would be most beneficial to the entire community. Each map will undoubtedly have some admirable features. We suggest that those of you who are most civic-minded and most interested in city planning try to incorporate in a well-drawn plan the best of the ideas presented. After this has been done, make inquiries to discover what group in your locality might be interested in considering your suggestions. This might be a parents' organization, a civic council, or a city planning commission. Some of your parents might know of a group that would appreciate your suggestions.

Plan an Ideal Community

Have your dreams ever included thoughts about the ideal place where you would like to live? Most of us like to imagine ourselves in new or

210. COMMUNITY PLANNING *Art class*

Here students are shown working as a group on a plan they have made for the improvement of their community. Other students concern themselves with building a section of a model community. Notice the interesting features of the multiple dwelling: an L-shape and a projecting entrance accessible to both wings of the building.

251

211. ARCHITECTURAL MODEL *Student work*

strange surroundings, especially at times when we are particularly impatient with the conditions under which we live. Here, then, is an opportunity to be more than a dreamer; to be a person of imagination and at the same time capable of thoughtful planning.

First choose a piece of land for your new community. Decide on its physical characteristics: mountains, rocks, inland or seashore. What should be its principal industry; fishing, fruit growing, farming, or manufacturing?

Draw a general plan on paper to show the chief physical characteristics of the land: rivers, mountains, lakes, plains, and similar natural features. These can be shown in color. Now consider the general plan of the city. Is it to be based upon a series of concentric circles, with main arteries leading to a central hub, as is the case in Washington, D. C.? Are there advantages in a plan of this sort, and if so, what would you place in the center: your main industries, your shopping and recreation center, or all public buildings?

The gridiron plan, a system of main thoroughfares and cross streets at right angles, is very familiar to all of us. New York City and Montreal, Canada, are laid out on such a plan. Do you think that the gridiron plan makes it easy for traffic to move or that it can be successful only when it includes express highways for through traffic?

Are there advantages in a fan-shaped plan that uses a spot like a harbor for a focal point? Perhaps you might decide that your community should be broken up into a number of small separate communities, each complete in itself. Whatever your final decision may be, indicate it clearly on your map and include all areas to be developed as well as outlying districts to be kept undeveloped in order to prevent overexpansion.

Now for the Buildings

Before indicating buildings of any description upon your map, it is well to review in your mind some of the basic requirements of good community planning. They fall into certain groups. The first concerns the question of housing:

1. Every inhabitant in your community ought to have sunlight and fresh air. Is this possible if houses are placed in endless rows, either attached as in semiprivate dwellings or in a tightly sealed city block? Should not houses, whether designed for one family, or as a multiple family dwell-

212. HOUSES *Stuttgart, Germany, J. J. Oud*

These houses were built as far back as 1927 for people with small incomes. They were designed to meet the basic requirements of air, sunlight, and space for living in an industrial area. Many of the ideas incorporated in these early projects are to be found in those of the present day.

The use of glass in a variety of ways is characteristic of modern building methods. In these dwellings, glass bricks were used to make exterior partitions. Thus, each family gained greater privacy without being deprived of light and sunshine.

213. HOUSES *Berlin, Germany, Luckhardt and Anker*

214. L-SHAPED HOUSES *L. Hilberseimer*

Designers have tried various ways of planning the layout of one- and two-family homes. This example is an interesting departure from the usual block form and provides a maximum amount of sunlight. The second plan was designed with playgrounds, schools, and recreational buildings as the core of a community. Notice the provision for adequate space between each residential unit.

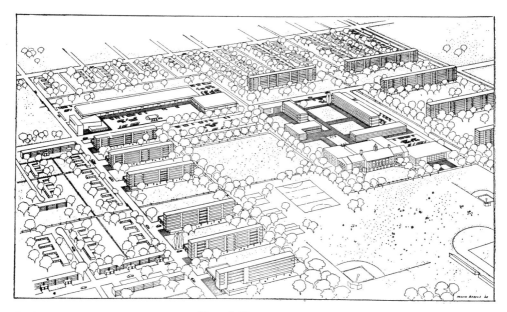

215. MODERN NEIGHBORHOOD *Frank Barcus*

ing, be so placed and arranged that there is ample space around each building?

2. Every inhabitant should have a view of something besides his neighbor's kitchen, back yard, or wash line. Does this not mean that apartments or private dwellings must not occupy all of their allotted land, thus insuring adequate space between buildings?

3. Communities should not be too large, nor should they allow too many people within one dwelling. Would you limit the size of your ideal community as well as the size and height of its buildings in order to preserve space for living? This is considered one of the essentials of community planning.

The second basic consideration of good community planning concerns the placing of public buildings and the allotment of land for public use:

1. Public buildings include the following: post office, courthouse, and library; hospital, church, school, and recreation center; travel terminals. They should be so situated that they are reached quickly and easily by all.

2. A shopping center should be composed of the necessary stores, grouped for the convenience of the community.

3. Each community should be properly provided with open land for parks and for recreation centers which contain tennis courts, baseball diamonds, swimming pools, and similar facilities.

The third, and highly important consideration, is the planning of traffic.

1. Main highways should be confined to certain designated roadways so that the residential sections may be free from the dangers and the discomforts associated with it.

2. Streets should be so planned that each vista, or view, is pleasant and stimulating.

Develop Your Plan

With black ink or crayon, draw lines on your plan to show the direction of roads, and of the railroads entering and crossing your community. Indicate main traffic ways by making them wider or darker than the others.

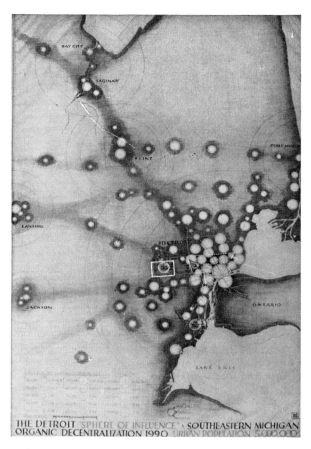

THE DETROIT SPHERE OF INFLUENCE : SOUTHEASTERN MICHIGAN
ORGANIC DECENTRALIZATION 1990 URBAN POPULATION 5,000,000

216. THE DETROIT AREA *J. Davidson Stephen*

This map-diagram might be compared with an aerial photograph taken at stratospheric altitudes and with a camera having infra-red equipment and film. It is an over-all view of the region.

Communities comprising the region are shown by small clustered circles. These small circles indicate the living area required for these communities. Variation in size of circles indicates a corresponding variation in the population of these communities.

Detroit's city limits are shown by the irregular shape (dotted lines) near the center of the map. Note that the city area of Detroit is composed of several communities or sub-communities (neighborhoods).

Plymouth, Michigan, a separate adjacent community, is shown by a small circle (dotted line) within a rectangular block (solid lines). Illustration 218 will show a more detailed study of Plymouth.

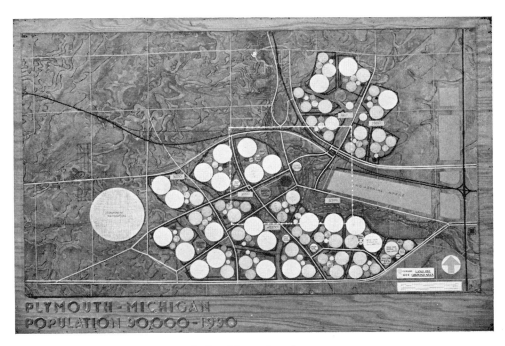

217. PLYMOUTH, MICHIGAN   *J. Davidson Stephen*

This model might be said to be an air-view at a much lower altitude than that of illustration 216. Differences in the geographical features come into view. The nature of the terrain is shown by contours. Highways appear as white lines. Railroads are shown by black lines together with industrial areas (gray blocks) at the right-hand side near the railroad intersection.

Neighborhoods comprising this community are surrounded by heavy outlines. There are twenty-four neighborhoods. Each neighborhood is composed of several elements indicated by circles of varying sizes and colors. Each neighborhood consists of three large circles showing housing of various kinds and four smaller circles showing the neighborhood civic center (fire station, post office, etc.), the neighborhood shopping and amusement center, the elementary school, and the neighborhood playground.

Community facilities, such as the community civic center (city hall), community shopping and amusement center, and the central high shool are shown near the center of the rectangular area marked by dotted lines. This rectangular area also includes two neighborhoods; one at the upper left-hand and another at the bottom-center. Illustration 218, which follows, shows a three-dimensional model of the rectangular area within the dotted lines.

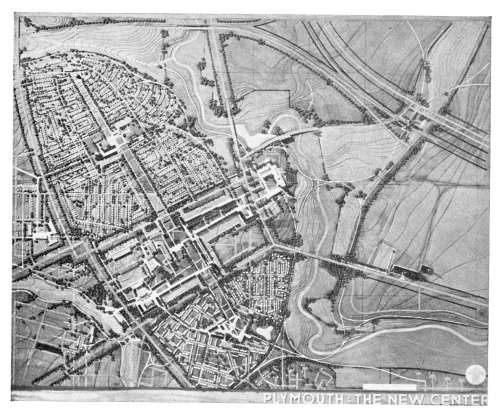

218. THE NEW CENTER OF PLYMOUTH, MICHIGAN   *J. Davidson Stephen*

This three-dimensional model is comparable to another air-view taken at a lower altitude than that of illustration 217. Now the individual houses and buildings and the trees come into view. The river can be seen meandering through the town. Highways can be clearly seen together with their green protective belts. These belts serve to separate the highways from the neighborhoods and from the community facilities shown at the center of the model.

The new center includes the community civic center, the community shopping and amusement center, and the new central high school designed for increased adult educational facilities together with adjacent parking lots serving all of these community features. The new railroad station is shown at the upper right-hand side. Lower, on the same side, a new industrial plant is located on the diagonal road that leads to the new center.

Two neighborhoods are shown. One neighborhood is at the upper left-hand side and the other neighborhood at the bottom center. A wide mall, connecting the neighborhood centers of these two neighborhoods, passes through the new center of Plymouth near the central high school. Each neighborhood has its own shopping and amusement facilities, its civic center, its recreational area, and its elementary school. Each neighborhood is conveniently near one of the junior and senior high schools.

258

Now mark in the public buildings, using a particular color, let us say red, to identify them. Yellow could be used to indicate the residential areas and green to map out the parks, lawns, and gardens.

As you work, imagine that you are an inhabitant of this ideal community. In imagination, walk down its streets; go to the school. Find the shops and from them carry your purchases to the house you selected for your own. Can you get about easily and have you seen pleasant sights along the way? Consider your friends who live, let us say, at the other end of the map. Will the plan be of equal advantage to them?

Compare Your Plans

Examine the plans made by your classmates and see how many of them have solved the community problem well. Make suggestions for improvement where necessary. Find and bring to class some pictures of communities planned by professional architects. You will find many successful solutions in communities throughout the country. Perhaps now you will begin to see how dreams may be realized through the courage and foresight of those who work to make them come true.

A Close-up View in Three Dimensions

Take a small section of your ideal community and develop it in greater detail. This section might be the school and its playgrounds; a park showing the plan and the location of the swimming pool, the tennis courts, the baseball diamond; a section of the residential area with gardens and walks. This plan might be carried out in a variety of ways. Perhaps you would like to make a three-dimensional plan, using blocks of wood, pieces of sandpaper, bits of sponge, and similar materials to represent your community. A flat plan could be drawn in colored inks or composed of colored papers, or you might prefer to make a very careful pencil drawing, to scale.

If enough students are interested, the plan for an entire community might be developed by having each one select and enlarge some section, all being careful to keep to the same scale and technique.

We Need Community Life

History shows that community planning dates back to the early days of long ago. The Acropolis in ancient Athens was a beautifully designed arrangement of public buildings and, in addition, provided adequate space for large gatherings.

We discover examples of all kinds of communities; some built for refuge about the stronghold of a ruler, such as we find in medieval times and others, such as cathedral towns, thickly clustered about a place of worship.

With a change in economic life came a change in the form and in the location of towns and cities. The automobile and the airplane have expanded trading and industrial areas and so made their mark on the location and form of communities.

The communities that have been planned are the ones of which the country and the inhabitants are most proud. To all Americans the great example of planning is the development of our National Capitol at Washington in the District of Columbia. From the time that President George Washington entrusted the design to the French engineer and architect, L'Enfant, a continuous plan has been followed. The Capitol, the White House, the Washington Monument, the Lincoln and the Thomas Jefferson Memorials, and many government buildings are joined by great avenues of parks. Reclamation of low-lying Potomac River lands made possible countless playgrounds, driveways and promenades. To see the city of Washington is to see a superb example of two of the greatest of man's qualities: vision and perseverance.

.   .   .

The language of art which you have now learned will remain with you always as a means of understanding the best efforts of mankind. It will enable you to enjoy the visible world and to appreciate even the most modest efforts of those who wish to improve themselves and their environment.

Your heart will grow as well as your mind, as you increase your understanding of art. Anyone who has a feeling for the beautiful will not overlook neglected people, places, or things. This awareness of beauty leads to constructive improvement of the world, in ever rising stages of civilization. With imagination each of us can help to build a finer world; with power each can work toward the realization of a more perfect state.

INDEX